A REAL LOOK AT REAL WORLD
CORPORATE GOVERNANCE

DAVID LARCKER

BRIAN TAYAN

A Real Look at Real World Corporate Governance
David Larcker and Brian Tayan

Editor: Michelle E. Gutman
Copy Editor: Diana Roome
Cover Design: Studio EM Graphic Design
Interior Design: Jocelyn Zada Chang

Permissions may be obtained by contacting the authors at:
corpgovernance@gsb.stanford.edu.
Published in the United States

First eBook Edition: July 2013
ISBN 978-0-9897101-0-7
First Printed Edition: August 2013
ISBN 978-0-9897101-1-4

A Real Look at Real World Corporate Governance
/ David F. Larcker, Brian Tayan.

TABLE OF CONTENTS

PREFACE

The contents of this book are the result of many years of diligent research by the authors. Our area of interest is "corporate governance," a broad field of study that involves organizational decisions made by the senior-most individuals of a corporation. These include:

- How do you assemble the *best* board of directors?
- How do you pick the *best* CEO?
- How much should a CEO *really* be paid?
- How do you *really* make sure the company is succeeding?

The list of questions goes on.

In the course of our study, we have noticed certain tendencies among the most vocal "experts" in corporate governance today. These include the tendencies to simplify decisions that are inherently complex, to prescribe uniform solutions to problems that are anything but uniform, and to be confident that their recommendations are correct when the evidence is anything but conclusive. We wrote this book, in part, to correct these tendencies.

In addition, we wrote this book for curious readers who are interested in corporations, how they are run, and how to make them better. You might be executives, directors, or employees. You might be investors, regulators, or other professionals. This book takes an honest look at the issues and decisions that really matter for corporate success and lays them out in a way that allows you to reach your own conclusions about what works, what doesn't, and why. In the end, it's your judgment—not the judgment of "experts"—that counts the most.

We would like to thank Michelle E. Gutman, our long-time researcher and close friend, whose unending effort underlies every page of every chapter in this book. Over the years, we have written many articles and papers, none of which would have been possible without her.

We would also like to thank the Rock Center for Corporate Governance at Stanford University, and the Center for Leadership Development and Research at the Stanford Graduate School of Business for their generous support of our research. Thank you to Diana Roome for editing this work and to Jocelyn Zada Chang for its design.

Lastly, thank you to Amy, Alexa, Sally, Sarah, and Dan—our wonderful families whom we love dearly.

INTRODUCTION

It never fails. Following every large-scale corporate collapse come calls for corporate reform. It doesn't matter whether the failure was Enron in 2001, the Penn Central Railroad in 1970, or the Knickerbocker Bank in 1907. The aftermath is the same: an insistence on the part of societal leaders and activists to do *something* to influence, curtail, or restrict corporate activity so that future crises are prevented and the damages they inflict avoided.

Today is no different. The bankruptcy of Lehman Brothers in 2008 — which nearly brought down the entire United States banking sector — elicited a chorus of governmental leaders agitating for change. To the White House, the problem was one of "greed and irresponsibility on the part of some." To the Federal Reserve, it was "misaligned incentives and excessive risk taking." To the Senate, it was a "lack of responsibility and accountability to shareholders." Consensus is that *self interest* nearly brought down the system and only a reduction in self interest would save the system in the future.

To achieve this, Congress passed a legislative bill that was monumental in both name and scope: the Dodd-Frank Wall Street Reform and Consumer Protection Act of 2010. Over 2,300 pages in length (35 times longer than the Sarbanes-Oxley Act of 2002), the law imposed rules and regulations impacting all aspects of the financial system, including banking, consumer credit, mortgage lending, derivative trading, insurance, and private partnerships. It also mandated a series of corporate governance reforms that applied to all publicly traded companies, regardless of industry or activity.

Dodd-Frank was not the end. No sooner was the law enacted than shareholder groups demanded new reforms beyond the act's scope. These groups sought changes to all aspects of corporate oversight, including the composition and workings of the board of directors, the size and structure of executive compensation, and the rights of shareholders to influence corporate matters. In the words of shareholder activist Carl Icahn, "Lax and ineffective boards, self-serving managements, and failed short-term strategies all contributed to the entirely preventable financial meltdown. It is time for battered shareholders to fight back."[1]

Unanswered in the debate are perhaps the most important questions of all: Will any of these reforms work? Is this the solution to the problem?

At least one prominent observer is wary. In a *New York Times* article, Professor Steven Davidoff of the Ohio State University Law School argues that while corporate governance reforms have the potential to improve the accountability of corporations to their shareholders, their ultimate success is unclear. He warns of "unintended consequences," including the unfortunate tendency of regulators and activists to emphasize "procedure over substance." He recommends that shareholder advocates study the effectiveness of their recommendations before compelling adoption. To this end, he calls governance "an empirical question."[2]

We agree. Corporate governance *is* a complex issue. Governance involves organizational decisions made at the senior-most level that directly influence the incentives, motivations, and behavior of all employees. These decisions are not easy to make, because it is not always clear *in advance* how structural and procedural changes will cascade throughout an organization to impact the dedication, drive, and honesty of its members.

We also agree that many of the so-called "best practices" promulgated today by governance experts have created an unintended emphasis on procedure over substance. While the problems of corporate governance might be obvious — repeated instances of accounting scandal, entrenched management, disengaged boards of directors, excessive compensation, and poor oversight — the solutions to these problems are not. As a result, the quick fixes that many experts have offered (and regulators subsequently adopted) tend to be superficial in nature. This has led to the situation in which we find ourselves today where the worst offenders check the boxes and claim compliance, while perfectly honest organizations continue to have to justify their unwillingness to conform.

In the long run, the best solution — indeed, the only workable solution — is to test various governance practices to see whether or not they work. Corporate governance is *empirical* in nature. Through standard social science tools (observation, objectivity, and measurement) we can learn which approaches are effective and which are not. This means that we do not need to resort to guesswork to advise corporations and their directors how to improve accountability and shareholder value, nor do we need to employ ideological arguments. We need to examine the research evidence, taking into account the idiosyncratic nature of each company's specific situation, and draw reasoned conclusions about the best courses of action.

This book is fundamentally dedicated to this approach. In the following chapters, we examine important governance issues through a lens that incorporates *both* research and experience. The conclusions are not always simple, but we believe this approach provides considerably more insight than theoretical arguments not grounded in fact. It also promises a new appreciation for the complicated issues that directors, managers, and shareholders grapple with each day.

WHAT IS CORPORATE GOVERNANCE?

Before we jump in, it is important to explain just what we mean by "corporate governance"—a term widely used but rarely defined. The theory of corporate governance rests on the idea that a separation between the ownership of a company and the management of a company creates the *potential* for management to take actions that further their own self interests, with the cost of these actions borne by shareholders. This is a classic economic problem, called the "agency problem." The phrase "agency problem" means just what the words imply: a problem that occurs when you hire another person to work on your behalf. We all know that agents—whether they are sales reps, real estate agents, or investment professionals managing your retirement account—care about their personal success as well as your own. Whether they take actions that are primarily in *your* best interest, *their own* best interest, or a combination of these is an important question that you will want to understand, but also a difficult one to predict in advance.

The same applies to the business world where the individuals running a business are not always the same as those who own the business. For example, imagine that you purchase the bar in your local town and decide to hire a manager to operate it on your behalf. This person is, in effect, your agent. If he or she works diligently to maximize profits, then you do not have much of an agency problem to worry about. If, on the other hand, this person takes cash out of the cash register, pours drinks for friends without charging them, undercharges patrons so that they in turn over-size their tips, or periodically takes bottles home for personal consumption, then you have a full-fledged agency problem on your hands. How you deal with this problem will depend on what solution you think is likely to work in a cost-effective manner. You might choose to add *control* systems, such as a cash register or inventory management system. You might choose to add a *monitoring* system, such as closed-circuit cameras or asking people you trust to periodically stop in to observe your manager's behavior. You might change the *incentive* system, such as offering your manager a percentage of the profits. Or you might make a *cultural* change, such as implementing a policy of only hiring people who are trustworthy in nature or highly ethical and then reinforce the importance of these behaviors through organizational routines (such as recognizing an "employee of the month"). The purpose behind these approaches is to forestall or reverse problems caused because the person managing the business is not the same as the person who owns the business. Not all of these approaches, however, will be cost-effective and as the owner you are interested only in adopting the ones that are.

The shareholders of large, publicly traded multinational corporations have the same concerns as the owner of the local bar, only on a much larger scale. The professional manager hired to run the corporation is an "agent" of the shareholders. The processes and procedures put in place to ensure that this agent works diligently to maximize profits are known as "the system of corporate governance." These might include control systems, such as inventory management or risk management protocols. They might include monitoring systems, such as a board of directors or an internal or external auditor. They could be incentive-based, such as a compensation system that includes performance bonuses. Or they might be cultural, such as an emphasis on ethical behavior and doing the right thing. What is clear in the corporate world, as in our earlier example, is that not all solutions are equally effective. Unnecessary or arbitrary requirements are likely to do more harm than good and, as Davidoff points out, can lead to a focus on procedure rather than substance.

HOW PREVALENT ARE GOVERNANCE PROBLEMS?

Unfortunately, everyday experience suggests that agency problems in the corporate world are a real problem that shareholders need to be concerned about. Because these behaviors are by nature concealed, and in some cases illegal, we can only estimate their prevalence. Approximately 8 percent of publicly traded companies each year have to restate their financial results due to previous manipulation or error. Approximately 10 percent of Chapter 11 bankruptcy cases involve allegations of fraud. And approximately 5 percent of publicly traded companies have been accused of retroactively changing the grant date of stock options to increase their compensation value to executives (so-called "stock option backdating"). These are severe cases of governance violations, and the frequency of low-level abuses — such as misuse of corporate spending accounts and small-dollar graft — are likely to be higher. According to a recent survey of financial service professionals in the United States and United Kingdom, 26 percent of respondents claim to have observed unethical or illegal behavior first-hand. Sixteen percent say they would commit illegal insider trading if they believed they could get away with it.[3] These are shocking figures that suggest agency problems are widespread and should not be ignored.

However, as we said earlier, recognizing the problem is not the hard part. Cost-effective solutions are the real challenge. Throughout this book we will examine a variety of topics, issues, and controversies in corporate governance. These include the obvious big-scale problems, such as financial manipulation ("cooking the books") and international bribery. They also include important "everyday" issues involving the composition of the board of directors, picking the right CEO to run the company, and designing correct pay packages for senior executives. Throughout, we will keep our attention focused on the fundamental big-picture question of which solutions work and which do not. To guide us, we will rely on empirical research and close observation. A superficial analysis will not suffice. Still, we warn you that these are complicated issues. Drawing sound conclusions will require sound judgment. It might also require changing prior beliefs. In the end, we hope that you are left with a greater appreciation for the problems that many large public corporations face and the types of solutions that do, and do not, fix them.

PART I:
BOARD OF DIRECTORS

The board of directors is the most recognized and central player in the corporate governance system. The board of directors is a group of individuals elected by shareholders to represent their economic interests and oversee management. The New York Stock Exchange (NYSE) requires that all publicly traded companies have a board—this is not discretionary—and the majority of the board's members must be "independent" of management (a term we will define shortly). For the most part, this is also true globally.

The role of the board is both to advise and to monitor management. These are two very different functions, and a qualified director is expected to do both. The dual nature of the board's mandate can create confusion among shareholders about exactly which decisions directors are expected to make and which they are not.

In its *advisory capacity*, the board consults with management regarding strategy and operations: which products and services the company should offer, in what regions or countries it should compete, how it should position itself relative to competitors, etc. Management proposes a corporate strategy to the board to address these issues, and the board tests the strategy by asking questions of management, pushing back, and raising important considerations—all with the purpose of ensuring that management's plan is the correct one to make profitable use of corporate assets and build shareholder wealth.

In its advisory capacity, the board acts *cooperatively* with management. Qualified directors are those who have relevant industry, functional, or geographic experience to advise on the issues at hand.

In its *oversight capacity*, the board is expected to monitor management and make sure that the executive team is acting in the best interest of shareholders. The board is responsible for such actions as hiring and firing the CEO, measuring corporate performance in relation to strategy, evaluating management contribution to performance, and designing the right compensation packages to attract, retain, and motivate qualified talent. The board also oversees legal and regulatory compliance, including the external audit, reporting requirements for publicly traded companies, and industry-specific regulations. To fulfill these responsibilities, the board typically relies on the advice of legal counsel and other paid professionals. In this regard, qualified directors are those who maintain *independence* from management and ensure that proper policies and procedures are in place and adhered to.

In short, effective directors are those who can cooperate and remain independent, as circumstances dictate.

What is Independence?

The concept of independence might seem straightforward. Independence is the ability of an individual to maintain perspective or judgment that is unbiased by a relationship with others.

But how exactly do you *regulate* independence?

According to the NYSE, an independent director is one with "no material relationship with the listed company." It defines a material relationship as one in which the director or a family member:

- Has been employed as an executive officer at the company within the last three years.

- Has earned direct compensation in excess of $120,000 from the company in the last three years.

- Has been employed as an internal or external auditor of the company in the last three years.

- Is an executive officer at another company where the listed company's present executives have served on the compensation committee in the last three years.

- Is an executive officer at a company whose business with the listed company has been the greater of 2 percent of gross revenues or $1 million within the last three years.

If these requirements seem arbitrary, they are. Why does $120,000 in compensation compromise independence but not $100,000? Why is business representing 2 percent of gross revenues "material"? Why is three years the relevant time frame beyond which independence is restored?

As in the case of all regulations, the line must be drawn somewhere and NYSE rules do just that. For investors, this means that mistakes will be made *on both sides of the line*. Some directors will meet the independence standards of the NYSE and not be truly independent in their judgment, while others will not meet these standards and yet be perfectly capable of maintaining independence from management.

Unfortunately, it can be very difficult for shareholders to determine which directors on their board are truly independent.

Another point that is often misunderstood is that the responsibilities of the board are not the same as those of management. Directors are expected to advise on managerial items such as corporate strategy and risk management, but not to develop plans and policies themselves. They are expected to ensure the integrity of financial statements but not to prepare the statements themselves. *The board is not an extension of management.* The board is a governing body elected to oversee management and represent the interest of shareholders. When companies fail (as many do), the board is accountable not because the board mismanaged the company but because the failure occurred under its supervision. We emphasize this point because it is difficult to diagnose the source of corporate failure and offer effective remedy without first understanding the proper roles of the board and management to understand which party (if either) made a mistake.

So why is it that so many boards end up overseeing failed corporations? What does it mean for a board to be "well functioning" and what attributes and processes are associated with "dysfunction"? How can shareholders tell in advance if their company has the right board in place to satisfy the dual obligations of advising and overseeing management? In the next three chapters, we will consider these questions from various angles.

1 LEHMAN BROTHERS: A CASE OF FORM OVER SUBSTANCE

A well-functioning board is one that makes informed and prudent decisions in the long-term interest of shareholders and stakeholders. It serves as an experienced advisor to management on issues ranging from strategy and risk management, to business and customer acquisition, to organizational design choices that involve productivity, employee motivation and retention, and culture. At the same time, it oversees both management and corporate performance and ensures that a broad range of regulatory and legal requirements are satisfied.

Given this, you might assume that a fairly standard set of guidelines exists that companies can follow to identify and recruit qualified directors to serve on the board. Unfortunately, it does not. Two things stand in the way. First, there is surprisingly little consensus — even among the so-called experts — about the standards that constitute best practices in board design. Second (and related to this), there is a tendency among those in a position to influence this decision to rely on their instincts about what practices *should* be best practices, without first looking at hard evidence to determine whether these practices are *in fact* best practices.

The problems that this creates are evidenced by the rules, regulations, and "best practices" that are prevalent today.

First, the rules and regulations. There is a long list of requirements that spell out how a board legally must be structured. For example, a majority of board members must be "independent" in accordance with the listing standards of the NYSE. The board must have standing subcommittees to oversee the audit function, executive compensation, director recruitment, and corporate governance. All members of these committees must be independent. In addition, all members of the audit committee must be "financially literate" and at least one must be a "financial expert."

Beyond these rules, companies are often pressured by outsiders to conform to an additional set of "best practices." For example, many experts advocate the appointment of an independent chairman (a chairman who is not also the CEO). An independent chairman is expected to bring counterbalance to the leadership of the CEO. Experts also frown on "classified boards" (boards whose directors are elected to three-year terms rather than the typical one-year term). Classified boards are thought to insulate directors from shareholder pressure. Experts also discourage "interlocked" boards (where an executive from Company A serves on the board of Company B while an executive from Company B serves on the board of Company A). Interlocked board members are thought to lack independence because of the reciprocal social linkages. Finally, experts advocate a series of standards relating to board size, diversity, and director compensation, all of which are intended to foster variety of perspective, accountability, and aligned incentives with shareholders.

Unfortunately, an extensive and very rigorous body of research says that most of these practices do not really matter. There is little evidence that independence standards — whether applied to the board, its committees, or its chairman — improve corporate performance or reduce the likelihood of failure.

A classified board structure can insulate directors from market pressure, but it can also protect a newly established company from takeover and allow directors to make decisions from a long-term perspective. Interlocked directors have the potential to lose their independence, but they also allow for superior information flows across companies that can be economically advantageous ("network effects"). Finally, the research shows that decisions about board composition can have either positive or negative impacts on group cohesion and decision making that are situationally specific and cannot be applied uniformly or blindly.

In short, most of the research says that most of the practices common in boardrooms today do not really matter or are too dependent on context to be generalized into a best practice.

That said, the evidence suggests that the *quality* of the board does matter — the expertise of its individual members, their engagement and dedication, and the manner in which they work together and with executives to arrive at well-informed decisions. The problem is, how can shareholders tell if they have a high-quality board? Two boards might look very similar in terms of structure but prove very different in effectiveness in representing and protecting shareholder interests.

THE BOARD OF LEHMAN BROTHERS

We can understand these issues better by considering the case of Lehman Brothers. Lehman is widely considered to have failed during the financial crisis of 2008 in part due to ineffective oversight by its board. Critics allege that the board did not sufficiently monitor the decisions of senior management or understand the financial and operational risks that the company was exposed to because of those decisions.

From a structural standpoint, there was nothing unusual about the Lehman board. It had ten directors, eight of whom met the independence standards of the New York Stock Exchange. Their average age was 68 years old (versus 61 years at the average large corporation). Directors were diverse in terms of their professional background, including a fairly typical mix of current and former CEOs, and executives from both for-profit and non-profit sectors. The directors at Lehman were not overly "busy" in terms of outside board affiliations. They were compensated with a mix of pay that included a healthy portion of equity (restricted stock units and options), as is advocated by many governance experts. In fact, from a structural standpoint, the board of Lehman Brothers was in many ways indistinguishable from the board of Goldman Sachs, a company that — while imperfect — certainly weathered the financial crisis better than Lehman. The table below compares the attributes of these two boards.

Board Attribute	Lehman	Goldman
"Classified?"	No, as of 2006	No, as of 2006
Independent Chairman	No	No
# of Directors	10	11
# of Current CEOs/ Chairmen	3	3
# of Retired CEOs/ Chairmen	3	2
Average Years Since Retired	12 years	3.5 years
# NYSE Independent	8	9
Independent Directors	**Current CEO/ Chairman:** - Red Cross - Glaxo - JDM Fin. **Retired CEO/ Chairman:** - Sotheby's - IBM - Halliburton **Other:** - Actress - Theater Producer	**Current CEO/ Chairman:** - Allstate - BP - Investor AB **Retired CEO/ Chairman:** - Sara Lee - Medtronic **Other:** - Perseus - Colgate-Palmolive - Brown U. - Asst. to President

Board Attribute	Lehman	Goldman
Average Age	68	59
Gender	Men: 8 Women: 2	Men: 9 Women: 2
# of Other Boards Currently on	19	17
Cash Comp.	$55,000	$75,000
Equity Comp.	$195,000	$260,000
# Board Meetings	8	7
# Executive Sessions	3	5
# Committee Meetings	Audit: 7 Comp: 8 Nom/Gov: 5 Fin/Risk: 2 Exec: 11	Audit: 11 Comp: 5 Nom/Gov: 5 - -

Source: Securities and Exchange Commission.

The failings of the Lehman board only become apparent when we look beyond its structural attributes and consider more subjective factors, such as the quality of professional background of its board members and their engagement in their responsibilities. For example, there is a notable absence of financial services expertise on the board. There is also an absence of current business experience. There were no current CEOs of major public corporations on the board in the years leading up to the crisis. The former CEOs on the board were well into retirement (12 years on average). This raises the question of whether the professional experiences of Lehman board members were relevant to understanding the increasing complexity of financial markets in the years leading up to the crisis. In addition, there is some question as to why the directors with nonprofit experience were recruited in the first place. In most corporations, directors with a nonprofit background tend to have academic or regulatory expertise that is relevant to the company's industry (for example, an academic research scientist might be recruited to sit on the board of a medical or pharmaceutical company). At Lehman, this does not appear to be the case. Director Roger Berlind was a theatrical producer, and director Dina Merrill a former actress.

Beyond the qualifications of the board, there is the simple question of how engaged directors were in monitoring the activities of Lehman management. This is a difficult assessment to make, especially given the lack of public information. From news articles, we know that CEO Richard Fuld was "aggressive, confrontational, blunt."[4] We also know that he tended to isolate himself from colleagues, taking a private elevator to

his executive suite. These might suggest that Fuld was a difficult executive to monitor. At the same time, there is evidence
that the board was not particularly structured to provide either
oversight of management or strategic advice. Instead, the responsibilities of the independent directors appear to be perfunctory. Theatrical producer Roger Berlind was appointed to
both the audit committee and the finance & risk committee,
where financial acumen is most critical. In addition, the finance & risk committee met only *two* times during the course
of the year. This is egregiously infrequent for a company whose
business model is fundamentally built on financial risk. The
compensation committee met more times (eight) than the audit committee (seven). The executive committee (which acts
on behalf of the board between meetings and has only two
members, including CEO Richard Fuld) appears to have been
more active than either the full board or the independent committees, suggesting that management had significant influence
over boardroom matters.

In the end, the substantive issues of board qualification and
engagement (rather than its superficial structure) very likely
contributed to Lehman's undoing.

KEY LESSONS. KEY QUESTIONS.
1. Investors, regulators, and governance experts place considerable emphasis on the structure of the board. Many boards are
   now indistinguishable in terms of regulatory independence,
   size, and personal and professional composition. However,
   the research evidence shows that the majority of these structural attributes have no proven impact (positive or negative)

on corporate performance and governance quality.

2. Has the emphasis on board structure led to homogenization of the board and a reduction in professional qualifications across companies today? Has oversight quality been compromised? At least in the case of Lehman Brothers, the answer appears to be yes.

3. In order for a board to provide proper advice and oversight to management, its members must be both qualified and engaged. They must also work together as a cohesive unit. How can shareholders gain better insight into whether they have a well-functioning and not perfunctory board? How can they ensure that the board has the right mix of expertise today, and that it has succession plans in place to ensure that it has the right mix in the future?

ARE CEOS THE BEST DIRECTORS?

By most accounts, the best directors should be those who are currently the CEOs of other corporations. Current (or "active") CEOs have an important mix of managerial, industry, and functional knowledge that equips them to advise and monitor other companies. They are uniquely positioned to gain the trust of and communicate with the CEO in a way that directors who lack this experience cannot. They can contribute to multiple areas of governance that are important for a firm's success, including development and vetting of the corporate strategy, risk management, internal talent development and CEO succession planning, performance measurement, and shareholder and stakeholder relations. They also have important intangible attributes such as leadership and decision-making skills, the ability to prioritize, the ability to lead in a crisis, and a strong work ethic. To this end, a survey by the National Association of Corporate Directors finds that CEO-level experience is the single most important functional background in recruiting a new director. Ninety-seven percent of respondents consider it "critical" or "important" professional experience when recruiting board candidates, a response rate far higher than for any other background.[5]

For these reasons, it is not surprising that some of the most visible CEOs in America serve on the boards of other large corporations. For example, Charles Moorman (CEO of Norfolk Southern) is on the board of Chevron, Patricia Woertz (CEO of Archer Daniels Midland) is on the board of Procter & Gamble, and David Cote (CEO of Honeywell) is on the board of JPMorgan Chase. CEOs who sit on outside boards indicate that they gain considerable insights from these experiences that benefit their own organizations.

Over the last ten years, however, the number of active CEOs serving as directors at other companies has declined quite precipitously. According to Spencer Stuart, active CEOs represented 41 percent of the pool of newly elected independent directors among S&P 500 companies in 2002. By 2012, that percentage fell to 25 percent. Active CEOs now sit on an average of only 0.6 outside boards, down from 1.2 a decade ago.

What accounts for this change? For one thing, more companies have adopted guidelines that limit (or prohibit) outside directorships for their current CEO. Almost three-quarters of companies now limit the number of outside board seats that their CEOs may serve on. These types of policies were not widely in effect a decade ago. Also, increased time demands — both from serving on outside boards and from being a CEO — likely encourage CEOs to voluntarily limit their directorships.

To compensate for this trend, companies have turned to recruiting new directors from the executive ranks below the CEO-level and also to recruiting more retired CEOs. The following table illustrates this trend.

Background of New Independent Directors	2002	2007	2012
CEO/Chairman	52%	47%	41%
Active	41%	33%	25%
Retired	11%	14%	16%
Other Corporate Execs	7%	21%	22%
Division Leader	2%	5%	12%
Line Leader	5%	16%	10%
Financial Background	21%	19%	22%
CFO/Treasurer	11%	8%	9%
Bankers	3%	5%	3%
Investors	2%	5%	8%
Accountants	5%	1%	2%
Other	20%	13%	15%
Academics/Nonprofit	6%	7%	7%
Consultants	7%	2%	2%
Lawyers	5%	2%	1%
Other	2%	2%	5%

Source: Spencer Stuart Board Index, 2012.

It is unclear whether the change in professional composition of corporate boards represents a reduction or an improvement in board quality. Currently, there is no widely accepted, rigorous study that demonstrates that current CEOs are better board members or that companies with CEO directors benefit in terms of improved advice or monitoring. In fact, some evidence suggests that active CEOs might *not* be the best board members. According to a study by Heidrick & Struggles and the Rock Center for Corporate Governance at Stanford University, 80 percent of corporate directors believe that active CEOs are no better than non-CEO board members. Although respondents value the strategic and operating expertise of CEO directors, when asked about their undesirable attributes, a full 87 percent believe that active CEOs are too busy with their own companies to be effective. See the following table.

Survey Results: Who Are the Best Directors?	
Are active-CEO directors better than average directors?	
Yes	21%
No	79%
Are retired-CEO directors better than active-CEO directors?	
Yes	55%
No	45%
Are retired-CEO directors better than average directors?	
Yes	47%
No	54%
How many years before CEO experience is outdated?	
<5 years	26%
5 to 10 years	20%
>10 years	16%
Never	38%

Source: Heidrick & Struggles and Stanford Rock Center, Corporate Board of Directors Survey, 2011.

To be sure, survey respondents identify several positive aspects of having active CEOs serve on the board. Beyond their strategic and managerial expertise, respondents value active CEOs for their experience dealing with crisis or failure, and for their extensive personal and professional networks. In terms of intangible attributes, active-CEO directors are seen as being able to identify with the CEO on a range of pressing issues, build trust with the CEO, prioritize challenges, and demonstrate current knowledge of business issues.

On the other hand, active CEOs are criticized for not being as engaged as the company needs them to be and for being unable to serve on time-consuming committees or participate in meetings called on short notice. Respondents also find fault with active CEOs for being too bossy, poor collaborators, and for not being good listeners.

The tenuous benefit of recruiting active-CEO directors is reflected in part in the research literature. Fahlenbrach, Low, and Stulz (2010) find no evidence that the appointment of an outside CEO positively contributes to future operating performance, decision making, or the monitoring of management by the board.[6] At the same time, research suggests that the appointment of active CEOs as directors might lead to increased CEO compensation. The Heidrick & Struggles and Stanford Rock Center survey cited above also found criticism of current CEOs for being "too generous with compensation."

For these reasons, it might be that the trend of recruiting fewer *active* CEOs and more *retired* CEOs as directors is beneficial to governance quality. After all, retired CEOs have similar strategic, operating, and leadership experience as current

CEOs but without the time demands that distract them from their director duties. According to the survey above, 55 percent of respondents believe that retired CEOs are better directors than active CEOs. However, as we saw in the case of Lehman Brothers in the previous chapter, there might be a time after which executive experience becomes so far outdated that it is no longer relevant.

KEY LESSONS. KEY QUESTIONS.

1. Many people believe that current CEOs are the best board members. However, there is no reliable research evidence to suggest that this is true. Active CEOs have the qualifications to be great directors; they just might not have the time to engage in their responsibilities. Companies might want to reassess the importance of this criterion when looking for new board members.

2. How much does the requirement for CEO-level experience limit the pool of available directors? Does this restrict the availability of diversity candidates who might be less likely to have that experience?

3. We saw in the case of Lehman Brothers a company that had a large number of retired executives. Is there a "shelf life" to CEO experience? Do the positive qualities of retired CEOs deteriorate, or do they never become outdated?

4. If the availability of current or retired CEOs is low, should professional directors (directors whose primary job is to serve on boards) be used to fill this gap? Professional directors offer the benefit of multiple company experience. However, like CEO directors, they might be too "busy" to engage

with each company they serve. Their reliance on board fees for income might also compromise their independence.

ARE THE DIRECTORS OF FAILED COMPANIES "TAINTED"?

In the previous two chapters, we have seen that, for the most part, the structure of the board does not matter while the quality of its members does. In this chapter, we examine a related question: should the CEOs and directors of failed companies be automatically disqualified from serving on other boards?

When a major governance failure occurs (such as a severe accounting restatement, unexpected litigation, or news of fraud or scandal), four things generally happen. First, the company's stock price immediately falls, with the magnitude of the decline commensurate with the perceived severity of the problem. Second, the stock tends to continue to underperform well past the announcement period, as the market weighs whether damage to the company is long-lasting. Third, the company and its officers and directors face lawsuits from shareholders and regulators, who seek to be compensated for their losses. And finally, there is elevated turnover in both the executive suite and the boardroom, as the company tries to signal to the market that it is serious about reform.

The impact on the long-term careers of the former executives and directors of these companies, however, is less clear. Recent experience suggests that many CEOs and directors of failed companies are able to retain outside directorships—and even obtain new ones—following their forced departures. For example, after resigning from Citigroup in 2007, former chairman and CEO Charles Prince was elected to the board of Xerox. Stanley O'Neill, former chairman and CEO of Merrill

Lynch, was not only named a director of Alcoa but was also appointed to that company's audit committee. As the following table illustrates, many nonexecutive directors at Lehman Brothers, Wachovia, Washington Mutual, Bear Stearns, and AIG retained or gained directorships after their companies failed.

Directorship Changes Following the Financial Crisis

	# Kept	# Added	# Lost
AIG			
Marshall A. Cohen	3	1	1
Martin S. Feldstein	1	-	-
Fred H. Langhammer	1	2	1
Stephen F. Bollenbach	3	-	-
Ellen V. Futter	2	-	-
Michael H. Sutton	1	-	1
Bear Stearns			
Henry S. Bienen	-	2	-
Michael Goldstein	3	1	2
Paul A. Novelly	1	2	-
Frederic V. Salerno	3	2	2
Vincent Tese	3	1	2
Lehman Brothers			
Marsha J. Evans	3	-	-
Roland A. Hernandez	3	2	2

	# Kept	# Added	# Lost
Wachovia			
John D. Baker	1	3	1
John T. Casteen III	-	1	-
Maryellen Herringer	2	-	
Robert A Ingram	4	1	1
Donald M. James	2	1	-
Mackey McDonald	1	4	-
Joseph Neubauer	3	-	-
Ruth G. Shaw	2	-	-
G. Kennedy Thompson	1	1	-
Dona D. Young	1	-	1
Washington Mutual			
Stephen I. Chazen	-	1	-
Stephen E. Frank	1	2	2
Charles M. Lillis	2	-	2
Orin C. Smith	2	-	-

Source: Securities and Exchange Commission, 2011.

Clearly, circumstances play a role in determining whether a leader of a failed company is fit to serve as director of other organizations. For example, an assessment might be based on the degree to which such an individual was associated with wrongdoing at their former employer. It might also depend on the individual's capacity to learn from error. In certain circumstances, a company might benefit from the knowledge and experience gained firsthand by an individual who was involved in a crisis or failure.

On the other hand, there are reasons why the executives and directors of failed companies might not be fit to hold future directorships. Governance failures are not the same as managerial failures. Executives are hired with the express purpose of taking strategic risk to increase shareholder value, some of which might not work out as planned. Corporate monitors, by contrast, are hired with the express purpose of preventing and detecting malfeasance. While "failure" is an anticipated outcome with a managerial job, it is not an expected part of a monitoring job. In addition, a governance failure might reveal underlying character flaws in the leaders themselves. If executives and directors were not sufficiently engaged in their duties (or, worse, if they were complicit or exhibited low levels of integrity), these shortcomings are likely to recur in other settings. Also, companies that retain such individuals in the future might be subject to heightened scrutiny. Rightly or wrongly, the leaders of failed institutions incur reputational damage simply through their association with a failed firm. Companies that subsequently employ them are likely to face strong pushback from shareholders and stakeholders who question why other, more qualified directors could not be recruited instead.

There is some evidence that the *executives* of failed companies are treated more strictly than the *directors* of those same companies. According to a recent survey of executives and directors, only 37 percent of respondents believe that the former CEO of a company that experienced substantial accounting and ethical problems can be a good board member at another company. By contrast, 67 percent of respondents believe that the directors of such a company can be a good board member elsewhere. When asked to elaborate, respondents explain that the CEO is held to a higher standard of accountability, given his or her position of leadership. Directors are presumed to have less involvement in potential violations and are also seen as able to learn from mistakes of this nature. These opinions, however, are not universal, as the following table indicates.

Survey Results: Are CEOs and Directors Tainted by Scandal?

"Can an ex-CEO of a company that experiences substantial accounting and ethical problems be a good board member at another company?"

Yes   37%
No   63%

Comments from respondents:

On the positive side…

> "The CEO may only know what he/she has been presented."

> "A good CEO learns why he missed the flaws, and does not drop the ball twice…"

> "As long as their integrity is not compromised, experience can be valuable/add a new perspective."

On the negative side…

> "As the CEO, he or she clearly must have had some lapse in leadership and oversight for there to be a substantial accounting or ethical issue in his/her tenure."

> "Ethical problems are not caused by a lack of knowledge, they are caused by character flaws (and character doesn't change)."

> "Even if they learned valuable lessons the reputational risks are too high and their credibility with other board members is a problem."

> "Once tainted, it is impossible to regain confidence in their integrity."

> "Tone at the top is a key driver of corporate culture, and the CEO is the most influential person in setting tone. Accounting and ethical issues are usually the result of problems with CEO performance."

"Can a board member (not the CEO) at a company that experiences substantial accounting and ethical problems be a good board member at another company?"

Yes   67%
No   33%

Comments from respondents:

On the positive side...

> "Assuming the board member was not involved in the irregularities, he or she should have learned valuable lessons from the experience."

> "Board members can be misled by management and learning to be skeptical from such an experience can make for a better board member."

> "Board members are more effective generally if they have experienced difficulties in their own careers."

On the negative side...

> "At the end of the day it is the board that shareholders place trust in, and they must have and show understanding of the company's accounts."

> "If it happened on their watch, you have to question how engaged they are in good governance."

Source: Heidrick & Struggles and Stanford Rock Center, Corporate Board of Directors Survey, 2011.

KEY LESSONS. KEY QUESTIONS.

1. In recent years, there have been many large- and small-scale corporate failures driven in part by ethical, accounting, or risk management improprieties. However, the executives and directors of these companies have in many cases gained or retained employment as directors of other firms. Should this be a concern for shareholders?

2. Executives and directors often suffer reputational damage from their association with a failed company. What is the standard by which their "culpability" should be judged? When are these individuals fit to hold future directorships, and when are they "too tainted" by their experience?

3. How plausible is the argument that an officer or director involved in an accounting or ethical problem "should have learned valuable lessons from the experience" that makes them a valuable board member for other companies? Can they be "redeemed" if they themselves engaged in bad behavior?

PART II:
ACCOUNTING AND CONTROLS

Along with the board of directors, the external auditor is another central player in the corporate governance system. The external auditor is a third-party firm (often one of the Big Four accounting firms) hired by the company to review its published financial statements and the process in which they are prepared.

Because shareholders rely on financial statements to make an informed determination of the fair value of a company's assets, the accuracy of these statements is critical. Shareholders expect—and NYSE rules require—that companies hire an independent auditor to review their financials and attest to their quality. Review by an objective, third-party auditor is intended to root out fraud or financial manipulation that an unscrupulous manager might engage in to inflate financial results or steal from the company. The presence of an external auditor discourages these activities by signaling that violators will get caught. (In this way, the hiring of an external auditor has a deterrence effect as well as a detection effect, similar to deploying highway patrol to be visible on the highway to slow traffic as well as issue tickets.)

However, for practical reasons, there are limits to this process that make it less foolproof than shareholders often hope or realize. Because of the massive size and complexity of corporate accounting systems, the external auditor cannot possibly review all accounts and transactions. The typical large multinational corporation has thousands of accounts and processes millions of accounting transactions each year. It would be prohibitively expensive to review all of these. To streamline the process, the auditor uses a sampling method, focusing attention on accounts that are at the greatest risk of inaccuracy. These include revenue accounts as well as accounts that rely heavily on management estimates, such as restructuring accounts, impairments, loss reserves, and allowances for uncollectible receivables. This still leaves plenty of room for an employee to manipulate results by avoiding scrutinized accounts and otherwise "gaming" the audit process.

Second, as much as shareholders would like the external auditor to conduct its review entirely independent of management, it cannot practically do so. Because of the complexity of corporate operations, an internal discussion is often required for auditors to understand why particular decisions are arrived at. While critics allege that this relationship can be "co-opted" (which it can), any successful audit must entail give-and-take communication between the professionals who prepare the accounts and those who review them. Still, auditors are expected to maintain "professional skepticism" throughout their engagement to ensure that their objectivity is not compromised over time.

Third, the audit process can be less than foolproof because, contrary to popular belief, there is no such thing as "correct" accounting. Accounting standards in the U.S. allow considerable flexibility to companies in the way in which they interpret and apply accounting standards. Accounting authorities allow this because it is not always clear how transactions should be valued or when the costs and revenues associated with a transaction should be recognized. Sometimes these decisions require discretion, and U.S. accounting standards allow just that. As a result, it can sometimes be difficult to discern "proper" accounting from "improper" accounting. Management might be simply aggressive or conservative. For this reason, the auditor does not provide assurance that accounting results are correct. Instead, the auditor merely expresses an *opinion* that the company's financial results are "presented fairly" in accordance with accounting rules. Effectively, the auditor tells shareholders that it did not find anything materially wrong with the computations leading to the financial statements (which is valuable in and of itself), but it does not promise that a material misstatement has not occurred.

For these reasons, there can be room for a manager or employee intent on manipulating results to do so without detection, so long as this person knows how to cover his or her tracks without detection. As the following table on financial restatements demonstrates, malfeasance can occur in practically any corner of the company.

Reasons for Financial Restatements: 2004-2008	Frequency
Revenue Recognition	10%
Expense Recognition	22%
Misclassification	18%
Equity	6%
Other Comprehensive Income	8%
Tax Accounting	11%
Acquisitions / Investments	6%
Capital Assets	6%
Inventory	3%
Reserves / Allowances	3%
Liability / Contingencies	3%
Other	3%

Source: Adapted from Mark Grothe and Poonam Goyal, Trend Report Restatements, Glass Lewis & Co. 2009.

So how do companies ensure that their accounts are properly kept and that management is not cooking the books? Can shareholders really rely on the financial results they receive? When manipulation or fraud does occur, how exactly do managers get away with it? What steps can companies take to try to prevent these occurrences? In the following three chapters we will explore these questions.

WHAT'S WRONG WITH GAAP? 4

Reliable financial reporting is essential to the proper functioning of capital markets. Investors rely on financial statements to make investment decisions and to evaluate the performance of management and companies. When reporting quality suffers — either because reported figures are inaccurate or because the company lacks transparency — assets become much more difficult to value, investors find themselves unable to properly assess risk and reward, and capital market efficiency declines. To prevent this, accounting authorities in the United States have established a set of accounting principles known as GAAP (or, "generally accepted accounting principles") that dictate how companies are expected to record business transactions.

Despite the rigor of the U.S. accounting system, companies still retain considerable discretion over financial reporting. They might decide to be conservative or aggressive in their application of accounting standards. Or they might decide to be more or less transparent with the information that they disclose to the public. (After all, competitors as well as shareholders look at these numbers.) Decisions on accounting quality are made by management, with approval from the audit committee of the board, and have a considerable impact on the quality of information conveyed to owners.

In recent years, some managers have taken this discretion one step further by publishing supplementary financial metrics (known as "non-GAAP" metrics) along with their official results. Non-GAAP metrics — also referred to as "core," "pro forma," "operating," or "adjusted" results — exclude certain income statement or balance sheet items that are required under

GAAP. These tend to be non-cash items such as restructuring charges, asset impairments, and amortization of intangibles. They might also include realized gains or losses on asset sales, or mark-to-market changes on securities that the company intends to hold to maturity. Management may prefer non-GAAP metrics because it believes the exclusion of these items provides a more relevant basis for measuring company performance during a specific reporting period. It might also prefer non-GAAP metrics because they paint a rosier picture of results. Not surprisingly, non-GAAP earnings tend to be higher than GAAP earnings.

Accountants and regulators have long been concerned that the use of non-GAAP financial metrics is abused by management to mislead investors and overstate earnings. To discourage this practice, the Sarbanes-Oxley Act of 2002 added restrictions to their use. Whenever a company reports a non-GAAP metric, it must also disclose the most directly comparable GAAP figure and provide a table that reconciles the two. Still, a large percentage of the companies in the Dow Jones report non-GAAP earnings, as the following table demonstrates.

Company	Non-GAAP EPS?	2009 Impact
3M	Yes	+ 4%
Alcoa	No	-
American Express	No	-

Company	Non-GAAP EPS?	2009 Impact
AT&T	No	-
Bank of America	No	-
Boeing	No	-
Caterpillar	Yes	+ 52%
Chevron	No	-
Cisco Systems	Yes	+ 29%
Coca-Cola	Yes	+ 4%
DuPont	Yes	+ 6%
Exxon Mobil	Yes	- 1%
General Electric	No	-
Hewlett-Packard	Yes	+ 15%
Home Depot	Yes	+ 7%
Intel	Yes	+ 52%
IBM	No	-
Johnson & Johnson	Yes	+ 5%
JPMorgan Chase	No	-
Kraft Foods	No	-
McDonald's	No	-
Merck	Yes	- 42%
Microsoft	No	-
Pfizer	Yes	+ 64%
Procter & Gamble	Yes	+ 3%
Travelers	No	-
United Technologies	No	-
Verizon	Yes	+ 86%
Wal-Mart Stores	Yes	- 2%
Walt Disney	Yes	+ 3%

Source: Company press releases.

The discrepancy between these metrics is not insignificant. Take, for example, Pfizer. Over the ten-year period 2000-2009, the company reported cumulative earnings per share of $18.51 on an adjusted basis. On a GAAP basis, cumulative earnings per share were only $12.68, a difference of 46 percent.

Year	GAAP EPS	Non-GAAP EPS	Difference
2009	$1.23	$2.02	64%
2008	$1.20	$2.42	102%
2007	$1.20	$2.20	83%
2006	$2.66	$2.06	-23%
2005	$1.09	$2.02	85%
2004	$1.49	$2.12	42%
2003	$0.54	$1.75	224%
2002	$1.46	$1.59	9%
2001	$1.22	$1.31	7%
2000	$0.59	$1.02	73%
Cumulative	$12.68	$18.51	46%

Source: Securities and Exchange Commission.

The practice has become so engrained that securities analysts *expect* companies to exclude one-time charges. For example, in July 2010, auto-supplier Johnson Controls announced earnings that narrowly missed consensus expectations by a penny a share, sending its stock down 5 percent. If it had adjusted for one-time costs, the company would have exceeded expectations. When asked by an analyst why the company had not excluded these items in order to meet expectations, the company's CFO replied, "I think we're going to be transparent in terms of when we have these types of costs, but we want to get away from pulling out all these things and saying just look at this or look at that. [...] We are going to be transparent when we have them, both good and bad, but we want to steer away from a lot of non-GAAP adjustments."[7]

Despite the potential for abuse, there is considerable evidence that certain non-GAAP earnings have higher information content than GAAP earnings.[8] Non-GAAP earnings are seen as more permanent than GAAP earnings in that they strip out one-time charges that are unlikely to recur. As such, they may provide better indication of the future earnings power of a company. For this reason, Wall Street analysts tend to forecast earnings estimates using non-GAAP metrics. Similarly, investors tend to value companies on this basis. For example, in 2008, Berkshire Hathaway entered into a series of long-duration derivative contracts whereby it promised to make payments to third parties if certain stock market indices traded below agreed-upon values on specified dates ranging from 2018 to 2028. The aggregate notional value of these contracts was $38 billion. GAAP requires such derivatives to be valued on a mark-to-market basis, meaning that their entire change in value is included in current net income even though the contracts specify that they cannot be exercised until expiration. As such, CEO Warren Buffett warned shareholders that the company's quarterly earnings would be subject to "wild swings." To improve transparency, the company would "continue to separate out these figures (as we do realized investment gains and losses) so that you can more clearly view the earnings of our operating businesses."[9] In the first quarter 2009, the derivative portfolio had a mark-to-market loss of $1.5 billion. The next quarter, it had a gain of $2.4 billion. By comparison, the operating businesses reported relatively stable net income of $1.7 billion and $1.8 billion in those quarters, respectively.

Other accounting principles have the potential to distort corporate earning power. For example, GAAP requires companies under certain circumstances to take mark-to-market gains or losses on the value of their own corporate debt, based on changes to its fair value. Ironically, the rules state that when a company's credit quality *deteriorates* such that its bonds decrease in value, the company should record a *gain* because it has the potential to repurchase those bonds in the open market at a discount. (This is ironic because companies that suffer a decrease in credit quality tend not to have the free capital necessary to make repurchases.) Likewise, the company would record a loss on its bonds when its credit quality improves and its bonds trade at higher values. During 2008, Morgan Stanley recorded a $5.3 billion gain when the market value of its bonds plummeted during the financial crisis. The next year, the company recorded a $5.5 billion loss when the value of those bonds recovered.

KEY LESSONS. KEY QUESTIONS.
1. The quality of financial accounting is critical to the prop-

er functioning of capital markets. It also aids the corporate governance process by allowing investors to closely monitor management and corporate performance. What does it say about the quality of the system that so many companies report non-GAAP earnings?

2. The passage of Sarbanes-Oxley was expected to decrease the prevalence of non-GAAP adjustments. Although it has succeeded in improving disclosure about their calculation, these metrics continue to be widely used. Who is driving this decision: the board, management, or the investment community? How can investors be sure that these adjustments are being made for their benefit and not to distort results?

3. Companies commonly make adjustments to income figures when determining management performance bonuses. Are the same non-GAAP measures used for bonuses as those reported to the market? If not, why not?

5 ROYAL DUTCH SHELL: A SHELL GAME WITH RESERVES

As we saw in the previous chapter, companies routinely make decisions that impact the quality of their accounting results. However, regardless of whether the path they choose is aggressive or conservative, their decisions are disclosed to shareholders and the numbers they report are reconciled to prevailing accounting standards. Shareholders can interpret these numbers for themselves and decide the extent to which they require adjustment. Even when management pushes the boundaries of accounting quality for self-serving purposes, the disclosure that allows shareholders to properly value their holdings is still available.

Outright financial fraud is an entirely different story. Fraud involves the intentional manipulation of published accounting results with the purpose of deceiving investors. Usually management commits fraud to inflate the value of bonuses or to boost the company stock price so they can sell stock or exercise options at artificially high prices. In some cases, fraud occurs for reputational gain (management enjoys the media attention that comes with large-scale success). Unfortunately for investors and regulators, no one really knows the frequency with which accounting manipulation occurs. Shareholders tend to learn about fraud only after it has been made public, either from a whistleblower who has come forward or when the situation becomes so untenable that it unravels (think, Enron). To date, researchers have not been able to construct models that predict accounting fraud with a high level of precision.

Most wide-scale accounting frauds share a few commonalities. First, they involve the active participation of leadership. Fraud is an *intentional* deception of the public, and it is difficult for a mid-level employee to engage in significant accounting fraud without management's knowledge and consent. (One exception involves trading fraud in large financial institutions where a single trader bypasses risk controls without management detection.) Second, accounting fraud involves multiple failures of the governance system. The board, auditors, the media, analysts, shareholders and regulators all fail to detect management misbehavior, either due to deficient control mechanisms; because governance participants fail to follow proper procedure; or because they do not subject company activity to an appropriate level of objective scrutiny. Third, there is a cultural element to fraud. Wide-scale accounting fraud involves daily actions of dubious or unethical quality. In a healthy organization such actions are witnessed and reported, but in a fraudulent organization unaffiliated employees turn a blind eye and allow misbehavior to persist. Fourth, fraud escalates over time. What might have started as an isolated occurrence evolves over time to become repeated and systemic.

To understand how financial fraud takes root in an organization, we will consider the case of Royal Dutch Shell. In 2004, Royal Dutch publicly admitted to overstating its proved oil reserves by an astonishing *4.5 billion barrels*, which represented 23 percent of total reserves. It was an embarrassing admission for a company that long prided itself on a reputation for expert management, disciplined strategic planning, and a culture of conservatism. How did such an error occur at a company so widely respected? As we will see, the accounting manipulation at Royal Dutch pretty much unfolded according to the script above. By examining its details, we can better understand how a series of governance and leadership failures that start small can cascade over time to create a colossal problem for an organization and its stakeholders.

CORPORATE STRUCTURE

Several factors contributed to the accounting problems at Royal Dutch — some organizational, some cultural, and some managerial. Organizationally, Royal Dutch Shell had a rather peculiar corporate structure. When the organization was formed in 1907 through the combination of the Royal Petroleum Company of the Netherlands and the Shell Transport and Trading Company of the United Kingdom, the companies did not structure the alliance as an outright merger. Instead, Royal Dutch and Shell remained separate legal entities, with separate headquarters, separate shareholders, and separate boards of directors. Only the operating interests of the two companies were combined. What by all rights should have been a single corporate entity instead had duplicate systems of oversight, as the following diagram illustrates.

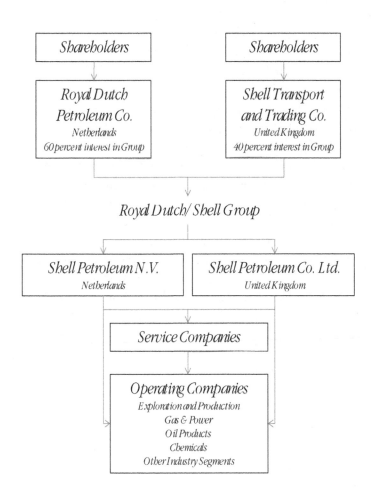

Source: Royal Dutch Petroleum Company, 2003 Annual Report.

This unique organizational structure required considerable coordination among corporate leaders. The boards of Royal Dutch and Shell Transport were *each* responsible for the appointment of management, the review and approval of financial statements, and the payment of dividends to shareholders. They were also each responsible for issues relating to strategy, investments, compensation, financial accounting and controls, and risk management. To coordinate advice and oversight, many of these activities were monitored through joint committees (committees with members from both boards).

Further complicating the situation was the fact that the operations of Royal Dutch Shell were not managed by a single CEO but by a committee of executives. The committee, known as the committee of managing directors (CMD), included executives from both companies and was jointly responsible for strategic and operating decisions. Members of the CMD were appointed by the boards of the two parent companies.

CORPORATE CULTURE

The second contributing factor to the Royal Dutch Shell accounting scandal was cultural. For decades, Royal Dutch had a culture that emphasized operational excellence and disciplined investment. Its central offices were world-renowned for careful and insightful planning. The group's sophisticated "scenario planning" techniques were famous for helping the company to side-step many of the problems that plagued the industry over time. For example, in the 1970s, the group foresaw the potential for an oil shock and moved to position itself in advance of higher prices. In the 1980s, it took a cautious position and insulated itself from an oil price collapse. In addition to planning, the company was esteemed for its engineering prowess, development of advanced technologies, and strict cost management.

Royal Dutch also had a culture that emphasized internal talent development. All leaders were promoted from within, and CMD members had extensive on-the-ground experience running local operations in dispersed parts of the world. In the words of Lodewijk van Wachem, chairman of the CMD from 1985 to 1992, "We have been able to steer our own course. This is certainly a function of the people, but the organizational structure helps.... We grow our own timber."[10] Furthermore, all major decisions were made on a consensus basis among CMD members. Decisions were less dependent on the judgment of one individual and benefited from the long experience of seasoned executives. Because decision making was institutionalized, it could more easily be passed on to future leaders as chairmanship of the CMD changed.

However, in the 1990s and early 2000s, persistently low oil prices put new pressure on the group to boost operating efficiency as it became increasingly difficult to profitably replace oil reserves with new investment. The changes that Royal Dutch made had the unintended consequence of also impacting its culture. First, the CMD rearranged group activities by business rather than geography. The change meant decreased autonomy for regional leaders who previously had extensive control over all activities in their territories, from exploration to retail gasoline sales. Activities that previously required the shared involvement of regional leaders were concentrated under a single set of leaders that had sole responsibility worldwide. This reduced the flow of information across groups. Second, the company's internal talent development process was revamped. Rather than maintain a rigid system of job rotation, the company migrated toward a more free-flowing internal labor market. This lessened the rigorous standards that historically underpinned management training and development. Third, corporate controls were relaxed, and employees were asked to define new ways of operating. This too weakened historically strong standards. Finally, management put renewed emphasis on growth. According to Cornelius Herkstroter, chairman of the CMD from 1993 to 1997: "The growing 'cash mountain' [on our balance sheet] is an indictment of our collective failure to bring forward sufficient investment or acquisition opportunities."[11] Mark Moody-Stuart, Herkstroter's successor who chaired the CMD from 1998 to 2001, reiterated this message: "If you don't deliver on the sort of things we've been promising the markets, you're dead."[12] "What is inescapable," he said, "is that we have allowed the competition to overtake us."[13] These changes to the company culture had the cumulative effect of loosening the company's once-strict standards of operational excellence and disciplined investment.

CORPORATE LEADERSHIP

Company leadership was a third contributing factor to the Royal Dutch Shell accounting scandal. In 2001, Philip Watts was named chairman of the committee of managing directors. Watts joined Shell in 1969 as a seismologist, geophysicist and exploration manager. Throughout his career, he took assignments in Southeast Asia, Africa, Europe, and the Middle East. In 1997, he became chief executive of exploration and production, the largest of Royal Dutch Shell's five global business units and responsible for finding new oil reserves.

Watts was known as a strong-willed executive who put intense pressure on subordinates to meet operating targets. In particular, Watts set an unrealistic goal that the company would achieve an oil reserve replacement ratio of 100 percent. A reserve replacement ratio above 100 percent was viewed positively by investors because it indicated that a company was successful in replacing the oil it produced each year with an equal amount of oil from new reserves. At the time, the company's reserve replacement ratio was below 80 percent due to the low pricing environment. Nevertheless, Watts promised investors that the company would get back to 100 percent and he instructed Walter van de Vijver (head of exploration and also a member of the CMD) to deliver on that target. It was this promise that ultimately pushed executives to manipulate the company's estimates of proved oil reserves.

PROVED OIL RESERVES

Proved oil reserves are the amount of oil that a company holds in underground reserves but has not yet produced. In order for reserves to be classified as "proved," they must be economically recoverable at current market prices. If not, they are given a lesser designation — either "possible" or "probable" — indicating that they will become producible only if oil prices climb or extraction technology advances. Although proved oil reserves are not reported on a company's balance sheet, companies are required by all major stock exchanges to disclose this figure, as it is an important indicator of future profitability.

Reserves are estimated based on the size of a reservoir, its physical properties, and the amount of the reservoir assumed to be recoverable. Because estimates are subject to discretion, experts examining the same reservoir can reasonably come to different conclusions about how much oil is "recoverable." The Society of Petroleum Evaluation Engineers recommends that engineers select the most conservative estimate. Importantly, reserve calculations are not audited by the external auditor because their calculation is not deemed reliable enough to justify an auditor's opinion.

Still, reserve restatements of the magnitude that occurred at Royal Dutch Shell are extremely rare and the degree of a typical reclassification ranges from only 1-5 percent. According to Lynn Turner, former chief accountant at the Securities and Exchange Commission (SEC), "A 20 percent restatement of proven reserves is a humongous error. For a company like Shell to have missed its proven reserves by that much is not an oversight. It's an intentional misapplication of the SEC's rules."[14] So how did it happen?

RESERVE MANIPULATION

On January 9, 2004, Royal Dutch Shell announced the first of what would ultimately turn out to be four downgrades of proved reserves. By the time the fourth reserve reduction was announced in May of that year, Royal Dutch had reduced its calculation of proved reserves by 23 percent, or 4.47 billion barrels.

To understand what happened, the Royal Dutch Shell group audit committee (GAC) commissioned U.S. law firm Davis Polk & Wardwell to perform an independent review of the events and background leading up to the restatement. The final report totaled 463 pages and exposed detailed information about tense exchanges between Watts and van de Vijver with regards to reserve estimates. According to Davis Polk, management knowledge of the problem was evident as early as February 2002, when van de Vijver informed the CMD that clarifications issued by the SEC "make it apparent that the group guidelines for booking proved reserves are no longer fully aligned with the SEC rules."[15] He estimated that the company was potentially exposed by 2.3 billion barrels but stipulated that "work has begun to address this important issue." Van de Vijver did not communicate this information to the GAC or to the boards of Royal Dutch or Shell Transport.

In May that same year, Watts sent an e-mail to van de Vijver directing him to put additional effort into finding replacement reserves for those that would potentially be reclassified:

> You will be bringing the issue to the CMD shortly. I do hope this review will include consideration of all ways and means of achieving more than 100 percent [reserve replacement] in 2002... considering the whole spectrum of possibilities and leaving no stone unturned.

In July 2002, van de Vijver made a presentation to the CMD about the company's reserves. As minutes of the meeting made clear, the focus of the presentation was not on the reason the company was noncompliant with SEC rules but instead, according to Davis Polk, on management's plan to "manage the totality of the reserve position over time, in hopes that problematic reserve bookings could be rendered immaterial by project maturation, license extensions, exploration successes and/or strategic activity." Minutes from the same meeting said that:

> It is considered unlikely that potential over-bookings would need to be de-booked in the short term, but reserves that are exposed to project risk or license expiry cannot remain on the books indefinitely if little progress is made to convert them to production in a timely manner.

In September, van de Vijver sent a memo to the CMD in which he described "dilemmas facing EP [exploration and production] and the uncomfortable situation EP is in":

> Given the external visibility of our issues… the market can only be "fooled" if 1) credibility of the company is high, 2) medium and long-term portfolio refreshment is real and/or 3) positive trends can be shown on key indicators. Unfortunately, … we are struggling on all key criteria.

Van de Vijver identified reserve replacement booking practices in previous years as a root of the company's current difficulties: "[Reserve replacement ratio] remains below 100 percent mainly due to aggressive booking in 1997-2000." Van de Vijver was implicating Watts, head of exploration and production during these years, for precipitating the problem, and yet the issue still was not escalated to the GAC or the boards of directors.

In November van de Vijver wrote to Watts: "I am becoming sick and tired about lying about the extent of our reserves issues and the downward revisions that need to be done because of far too aggressive/optimistic bookings."

In December, exploration and production staff advised

van de Vijver that he had a fiduciary duty to communicate his knowledge of the reserve estimates to the public. They wrote in a memo:

> *If... it is accepted or acknowledged by the management... [that] the 2002 proved reserves as reported in the Form 20-F [to the SEC] are materially wrong, the issuers are under a legal obligation to disclose that information to all investors at the same time and without delay. Not to disclose it would constitute a violation of U.S. securities law and the multiple listing requirements. It would also increase any potential exposure to liability within and outside the U.S.*

Van de Vijver responded by e-mail: "This is absolute dynamite, not at all what I expected and needs to be destroyed." Still, he notified the GAC of the problem, and the process began by which the company ultimately announced the revision in January 2004.

SOURCE OF RESERVE MANIPULATION

Despite these facts, Davis Polk did not identify a "common explanation" for the reserve problem. The firm noted that the process by which reserves were overstated varied region by region, concluding that "the booking of 'aggressive' reserves and their continued place on Shell's books were only possible because of certain deficiencies in the company's controls." The internal audit function was "understaffed and undertrained." It was "provided with virtually no instruction concerning regulatory requirements." Davis Polk also found that "Shell guidelines blurred the distinction between reserves reporting for internal decision-making and the requirements for regulatory reporting of proved reserves."

Davis Polk also blamed company CFO Judy Boynton for being "not effective" in her compliance function. In addition, it identified a lack of oversight by the board of directors: "Shell's outside directors and the GAC were not presented with the information that would have allowed them to identify or to address the issue."

In response to the report, Lord Oxburgh, nonexecutive chairman of Shell Transport, commented that "the committee had tried to get hold of the information [about reserves] for a long time but had failed."[16] He expressed a belief that the reserve replacement issue did not "have significance for the culture of the company as a whole." Instead, he attributed the problem to "human failings not structural deficiencies."[17] Watts and van de Vijver resigned at the request of their respective boards.

KEY LESSONS. KEY QUESTIONS.

1. Reserve estimates are not unique to the oil and gas industries. Practically every company books some type of reserve: insurance companies reserve for losses, financial institutions reserve for uncollectible loans, manufacturers and service providers reserve for uncollectible receivables. In all cases, best practices dictate that reserve estimates be independently verified by auditors, compliance officials, and the board of directors. How do these parties satisfy themselves that the estimates provided by management are reliable?

2. The problems of Royal Dutch Shell involve organizational, cultural, and leadership failures that developed over time.

How can the board of directors monitor an organization to ensure that undesirable changes do not "creep" in over time? How can shareholders gain better insight into the quality of culture and leadership within the companies they own?

3. Lord Oxburgh believed that the reserve problem lay in "human failings, not structural deficiencies." Are cultural failures "human" or "structural?" The answer to this question is important for the proper design of corporate governance solutions to accounting-related agency problems.

6 BAKER HUGHES: DE-CORRUPTING FOREIGN PRACTICES

The accounting issues at Royal Dutch Shell illustrate how a failure in organizational leadership and internal controls can, in time, precipitate a major scandal. This, of course, leads to the obvious question: *after a scandal occurs*, what can a company do to fix its problems? To answer this, we turn to the example of Baker Hughes.

Baker Hughes is a worldwide leader in drilling technology for use in oil and gas production. As an oilfield service provider, Baker Hughes does not produce these energy sources itself but provides goods and services to the companies that do. These include advanced drill bits, well logging services, directional drilling, drilling fluids and systems, and flow control equipment. Its customers include both multinational corporations such as ExxonMobil and state-controlled entities such as Saudi Aramco. Baker Hughes operates in over 65 countries, ranging from Angola to Uzbekistan.

As a U.S. corporation, Baker Hughes is subject to the Foreign Corrupt Practices Act (FCPA) of 1977. The FCPA is an anti-bribery law stemming from the post-Watergate Era that makes it illegal for a member of a U.S. corporation to offer payment to a foreign official for the purpose of obtaining or retaining business. While Baker Hughes has long had policies and processes in place to detect and prevent such an occurrence, it is not always easy to enforce these policies in the types of countries where Baker Hughes does business. About a decade ago Baker Hughes discovered *multiple* violations of the

FCPA within its operations. In this chapter, we will examine the steps that Baker Hughes took in response to this discovery. The company made changes to its operating principles that not only allowed it to become *compliant* with the legal and ethical standards of the FCPA but also to fundamentally *improve* the way it ran its business. The case of Baker Hughes illustrates that effective governance reform goes beyond minimum standards and requires a thoughtful solution that specifically addresses the problem at hand. In this way, we will see that the most effective governance solutions are commonly the most business-like.

FOREIGN CORRUPTION AND THE FCPA

Multinational corporations face a considerable risk of encountering corruption in developing nations. According to Transparency International, almost *40 percent* of executives in multinational corporations have been asked to pay a bribe when dealing with government and quasi-government offices. The incident rate is even higher (more than 60 percent) in poorer nations, such as Egypt, India, Indonesia, and Nigeria.[18] The dollar amount of bribes paid to politicians and government officials worldwide is estimated to be between $20 billion and $40 billion annually.

To reduce foreign corruption, the United States enacted the Foreign Corrupt Practices Act (FCPA) of 1977, which includes two main provisions. The anti-bribery provision makes it illegal for a U.S. corporation to offer payments to a foreign official for the purpose of "obtaining or retaining business" or "securing any improper advantage." The act creates an exemption for facilitating payments—payments whose purpose is "to expedite or to secure the performance of a routine governmental action," such as obtaining permits, processing visas, and similar transactions—which are not considered bribes. The books-and-records provision makes it illegal for companies to fail to "keep books, records, and accounts" that reasonably reflect the nature of transactions. This provision is intended to deter companies from burying illegal payments in generic accounts such as "travel and entertainment," "consulting fees," or "commissions." Of note, the FCPA applies only to company employees that offer or agree to pay bribes (the supply side). It does not apply to the foreign officials who solicit or accept bribes (the demand side).

The FCPA poses many risks to an oilfield services company such as Baker Hughes, operating as it does in oil-producing nations, several of which rank high on international corruption indices. Furthermore, many of its customers are state-owned oil production companies. The process of securing business contracts with these companies involves regular interaction with government officials and employees, any one of which might solicit an illegal payment. Because the FCPA does not specify a materiality threshold, even nominal expenditures that involve a government official (such as a token gift or entertainment expense) can potentially be construed as a violation. Once a service agreement is in place, Baker Hughes is under contract to deliver equipment on schedule, as delays to production are extremely costly. Because this equipment is imported, the company must routinely obtain clearance from customs offices where the risk of small-dollar graft is high. Even though facilitating payments are allowable under the FCPA, it is not always clear whether a payment is made to expedite a routine government service or is a bribe. Finally, like other multinational corporations, Baker Hughes has historically relied on third-party agents to help the company navigate regulatory bureaucracy. Because local agents are immersed in the local customs, it is not always easy to police their activity and ensure their compliance with the FCPA.

INDONESIA (1998)

In 1998, Baker Hughes faced its first violation of the FCPA. It began when the Indonesian ministry of finance informed a subsidiary of Baker Hughes that it was auditing a recent tax filing in which the company claimed a substantial tax refund. Following a preliminary review, the ministry reversed the company's tax refund and assessed a $3.2 million liability. Baker Hughes asked its tax accountant KPMG to review the report, and KPMG concluded that the finding was in error. In a meeting with KPMG, an Indonesian tax official asked that Baker Hughes pay a $200,000 "goodwill payment" in return for which the official would reduce the assessed tax liability. A regional tax manager for Baker Hughes instructed KPMG not to make the payment.

In a follow-up meeting, the Indonesian tax official offered to reduce the tax liability from $3.2 million to $270,000 in exchange for a lesser payment of $75,000. KPMG offered to make the payment on behalf of Baker Hughes and pass the charge through to the company by adding it to an invoice under the line item "professional services rendered." The regional tax manager for Baker Hughes discussed the matter with the company's controller and an FCPA advisor. The FCPA advisor concluded that the payment was not permissible. The regional tax manager continued to discuss the matter with the controller and argued that the payment would give Baker Hughes "certainty" over its taxes. The controller informed both the CFO and the general counsel of Baker Hughes of the matter. The general counsel agreed that the payment was illegal under the FCPA. The controller and CFO, however, disregarded his opinion and authorized the payment through KPMG. When KPMG generated the invoice, Baker Hughes entered the transaction on its books as professional services rendered. Shortly thereafter, the Indonesian tax official determined that Baker Hughes' tax liability was $270,000.

The general counsel discovered the authorization and intervened to stop payment on the invoice to KPMG. It also disclosed the matter to the SEC and the Department of Justice (DOJ). The employees involved—including the CFO and controller—were terminated, and KPMG was dismissed as tax accountant. Baker Hughes paid the Indonesian ministry of finance $2.1 million, which it estimated to be the appropriate tax assessment. Baker Hughes settled the matter with the SEC in 2001 and agreed to cease and desist from future violations.[19]

ALLEGATIONS IN NIGERIA (2002)

In March 2002, Baker Hughes discovered additional FCPA violations. This time, the events began when a former employee filed suit against the company alleging that he had been wrongfully terminated after refusing to pay a bribe to an agent in Nigeria. The employee had previously been division manager of BHI Inteq, a drilling subsidiary of Baker Hughes. In 1999, BHI Inteq bid on a two-year, $70 million contract to provide drilling services for the Shell Nigeria EA Shallow Offshore project. The project was managed by Royal Dutch Shell and jointly owned by Shell, the Nigerian National Petroleum Corp, Total, and Eni.

The employee alleged that he and a colleague had been approached by an agent who claimed to have an inside contact at Shell Nigeria. The agent offered to help BHI Inteq secure the contract if the company would share a percentage of the revenue with his firm. The division manager of BHI Inteq balked at the offer. Shortly thereafter, he was transferred to a project in the United States and terminated five months later. He alleged that his termination was due to the fact that he had refused to participate in the bribery scheme. BHI Inteq ultimately hired the agent in question and won the contract in 2001.

The allegations were even more severe than the Indonesian incident because Baker Hughes was still operating under a cease-and-desist order with the SEC. Further violations in such a case carry heightened penalties.

INTERNAL INVESTIGATIONS AND FINDINGS

Baker Hughes responded to the allegations by convening two panels to look into the matter. The first was a panel of independent investigators, led by a former prosecutor for the Department of Justice. Its objective was to focus on the events in Nigeria, determine what happened, and relay all information to the SEC and the DOJ as it was uncovered. The second panel comprised independent experts to review the investigative actions and advise the company on how to improve its compliance processes going forward.

When it concluded its investigation, the investigative panel found no evidence of illegal activity in Nigeria. It determined that Baker Hughes did not improperly terminate the employee who filed the grievance. Also, it found no evidence that Baker Hughes violated or attempted to violate the FCPA by making improper payments, either to the agent in question or to Shell. While the agent did have a brother who worked at Shell, there was no evidence that the agent used this relationship in an improper manner.

Still, the investigation uncovered several troublesome findings. Even though there was no evidence of illegal activity, the agent's behavior was clearly questionable. Large dollar amounts flowed through his agency with insufficient documentation to explain their purpose. Furthermore, there was not a clear business case for why he was hired by Baker Hughes. He did not have proven technical expertise, relevant experience, or connections with the local ministry. The company promptly terminated its relationship with him.

From a compliance standpoint, Baker Hughes had satisfied its obligations, and by all rights the matter could have ended there. However, senior management recognized that if the company had employed an agent of questionable merit in Nigeria, it was likely that a similar situation existed in other parts of the company. As a result, the company decided to *voluntarily* expand the scope of its internal investigation and proactively examine all agents that it employed. Several facts came out of this expanded investigation. First, Baker Hughes determined that its existing policy on the hiring of agents was not properly enforced. The policy called for a central list of agents, but none existed. The policy also called for division heads to keep background information on all agents in a repository that could be examined by internal auditors. This too had not happened. Second, the company discovered that there was insufficient justification for many of the agents that it employed. Because agents were paid a commission for their services, it was important that division heads be able to justify each on a cost-benefit basis. The advisory panel discovered that in many cases, this calculation had not been done. Third, Baker Hughes identified risks involving other types of agents such as processing agents, which were relied on to facilitate routine services such as visa acquisition, calculation of import taxes, and expediting shipments through customs. The activity of these agents had also not been closely monitored.

Furthermore, the expanded investigation uncovered additional violations of the FCPA in countries including Nigeria, Angola, Indonesia, Russia, Uzbekistan, and Kazakhstan. Many were minor incidences and did not involve a direct attempt by employees to pay or cover up bribes. In all cases these violations involved insufficient effort in monitoring agent behavior. For example:

• From 1998 to 2004, Baker Hughes authorized commission payments of nearly $5.3 million to an agent who worked in Kazakhstan, Russia, and Uzbekistan without adequately determining whether the payments were in part funneled to government officials.

- Between 2000 and 2003, Baker Hughes paid certain freight forwarders to import equipment into Indonesia using a "door-to-door" process without adequately determining whether the payments were being passed on to Indonesian customs officials.
- Between 2001 and 2005, Baker Hughes authorized payments to certain customs brokers to facilitate the resolution of alleged customs deficiencies without adequately determining whether the payments were being passed on to Nigerian customs officials.
- From 1998 to 2003, Baker Hughes paid an agent more than $10.3 million in commissions without adequately determining whether the payments were being passed on to employees of Sonangol, Angola's state-owned oil company, to obtain or retain business in Angola.[20]

That is, while Baker Hughes did not directly or indirectly participate in any attempt to bribe foreign officials, the company had failed to verify that its money was not being used for this purpose. One case, involving Kazakhstan, was more severe. Baker Hughes discovered that on two occasions, the company hired agents in that country with the express knowledge that some or all of the payments made to the agents were intended to bribe government officials.

Importantly, it was Baker Hughes that discovered each of these violations through the course of its expanded internal investigation and brought them to the attention of the SEC and the DOJ. Because of this, the DOJ recommended a reduced settlement significantly below federal sentencing guidelines. The federal judge who approved the settlement praised the company in language rarely used for a corporate defendant:

> *First, and most important, [Baker Hughes'] cooperation with the government has been exemplary. The willingness of [the company] to devote such substantial resources to its investigation, and the extensive voluntary disclosures of evidence uncovered by that investigation, shed light on the characteristics of the defendant and on the need for the sentence imposed to promote respect for the law. [Baker Hughes'] commitment to the ideal of responsible corporate citizenship, manifested throughout the investigation by its diligence and candor, is a significant mitigating characteristic and demonstrates that respect for the law is already ingrained in [Baker Hughes'] corporate values and culture.[21]*

GOVERNANCE REFORMS

The company used the findings of the internal investigation and advisory panel to implement a broad set of governance reforms to strengthen the company's underlying business. First, the company changed the process by which it hired agents. Before an agent could be hired, the division manager making the request had to submit a business justification and perform extensive due diligence to ensure FCPA compliance. If the request was approved, the division manager was required to monitor the agent over the life of the contract. A local compliance officer had to review all large-dollar payments (in excess of $20,000). Agents employed by the company were required to undergo periodic recertification and were subject to a comprehensive legal and financial audit at any time. If the agent failed to cooperate with these controls, he or she was terminated.

The new procedures not only improved FCPA compliance at Baker Hughes but improved the company's business operations. As a result of the new procedures, the number of agents employed by the company was reduced to less than *10 percent* of what it had been in 2002. The company also lost some business. Still, on the whole, the changes brought many benefits that more than compensated for these losses. Division managers knew much more information about the agents they hired because of the due diligence process. In addition, in the many cases where an agent was not hired, company employees developed closer relations with their customers because they worked directly with them rather than through an agent. This allowed the company to vastly improve its customer service and grow relations more profitably than it had previously.

KEY LESSONS. KEY QUESTIONS.

1. The case of Baker Hughes demonstrates the importance of internal controls in deterring and detecting inappropriate behavior. In order to be effective, control mechanisms need to do more than *restrict* activity. They need to be designed to work within the context of the company's business and operating environment to *promote* positive performance. In this way, proper risk management controls can positively contribute to company performance.

2. Even at their best, there is a limit to how effective internal controls can be. Controls restrict activity but they cannot prevent malfeasance. At some point, an awareness of correct behavior needs to be ingrained in the culture of the company. What steps can management take to evaluate the

"quality" of its culture? What steps can it take to "shape" or "improve" culture? What role does the board play?

3. The problems at Royal Dutch Shell and Baker Hughes both stem from violation of company protocol. They both involve disregard for internal controls. And they both involve cultural failings. At the same time, they also both required a *crisis* before internal changes were made. How can company leadership (either management or the board) take better action to prevent crises from developing in the first place? What metrics or data should it look at to determine whether internal changes should be made *now*?

PART III:
CEO SUCCESSION PLANNING

One of the most important decisions that a board must make is who to select as the chief executive officer of the company. The CEO is responsible not only for developing and implementing the corporate strategy but also for day-to-day oversight of its operations, the design of the organizational structure, establishing work processes, setting compensation, shaping culture, and motivating performance. To find the most qualified candidate for the job, the board must have an understanding not only of the skills and experiences required to lead the company, but also the necessary behavioral attributes such as ethics, cultural fit, work style, risk tolerance, competitiveness, and leadership. There are four general approaches to selecting a CEO:

1. *CEO-in-Waiting.* The company promotes a leading candidate to the position of president or chief operating officer, where he or she is groomed to eventually become the CEO. This approach allows the board to observe first-hand how an executive performs when given CEO-level responsibility before having to commit to the appointment.

2. *Horse Race.* The company promotes two or more internal candidates to high-level senior positions where they formally compete to become CEO. This approach allows the company to groom multiple executives before settling on a favorite.

3. *External Recruit.* The company recruits an executive from outside the organization. This approach is preferable when the company lacks qualified internal talent, or the company is in a turnaround situation that requires significant strategic, operating, or financial changes.
4. *Inside-Outside Approach.* The company combines a horse race with an external search. This approach allows the company to compare leading internal candidates against the external market and select the most qualified individual.

There are benefits as well as downsides to each of these approaches. Internal candidates offer continuity to the company and will have had their performance evaluated up close. The board will therefore observe first-hand their style of management, leadership, communication, skill, and drive. That said, most internal executives have never actually *been* a CEO. No amount of observation, coaching, and development will give the board 100 percent assurance that an untested executive can handle the complete responsibility until he or she assumes the role. This is where the allure of the external executive comes in. External candidates tend to have proven experience as a CEO, often within the same or similar industry. Their performance is on record and their leadership style known. However, board members tend to view external candidates through rose-colored glasses. They have not worked with them directly, and so they are less familiar with their flaws. External candidates are also well versed in making a good impression — particularly in an interview setting. This can bias board members in their favor, but until an executive is tested in a specific company there can be no assurance that the work style that made him or her successful in a previous company will translate well to a new environment.

Nevertheless, selecting the right executive for the CEO position is the board's responsibility and shareholders expect them to make the right choice. To do so requires having a comprehensive process in place to evaluate a set of executives thoroughly and objectively. Succession is a *process* not an *event*, and irrespective of the specific approach that the board chooses it is important that the process is managed well. The CEO transition can be distracting, with heightened scrutiny from both internal and external constituents. The choice of a successor also creates ripple effects one, two, and three levels below the CEO as other senior executives are transitioned, promoted to new responsibilities, or hired away by competitors if they are passed over. For these reasons, the board must put structure around succession planning to ensure that nothing derails it or impedes the company's performance during a transition.

In the following three chapters, we will take a detailed look at the CEO succession process. How successful are companies at selecting the right CEO? In general, are they well prepared for a transition? If not, why not? Would shareholders benefit if companies disclosed more information about their succession plans? What types of information should be included in this disclosure? Should companies disclose health information about their CEO if this helps shareholders to anticipate when a transition might take place?

As we will see, when the succession process goes awry, it can go *seriously* awry. Fortunately, we will also see that this is a preventable problem with the proper level of board engagement.

SUDDEN DEATH OF A CEO

Every year, approximately 10 to 15 percent of companies change CEOs. CEOs leave for a variety of reasons: they retire, they suffer from health problems, they are recruited to another firm, they are terminated for poor performance, or they resign following a takeover. The decision to change leaders can be the CEO's or the board's, or it can be thrust on the company by the market or life events outside anyone's control. For these reasons, a well governed company always has a plan in place to deal with both expected and unexpected transitions.

CEO Turnover	2002	2003	2004	2005	2006
Planned	5.0%	5.3%	7.7%	9.2%	6.6%
Forced	4.4%	3.2%	4.5%	3.6%	4.6%
M&A	1.4%	1.3%	2.5%	2.6%	3.2%
Total	10.8%	9.8%	14.7%	15.4%	14.4%

CEO Turnover	2007	2008	2009	2010	2011
Planned	6.8%	7.2%	9.1%	7.7%	9.8%
Forced	4.2%	5.1%	3.4%	2.2%	2.2%
M&A	2.8%	2.2%	1.8%	1.8%	2.2%
Total	13.8%	14.4%	14.3%	11.6%	14.2%

Source: Ken Favaro, Per-Ola Karlsson, and Gary Nielson, CEO Succession Report, Booz & Co., 2011.

Despite the importance of a succession plan, many boards are not prepared to replace their CEO. According to a recent survey, just over *half* of companies would be unable to name a permanent successor, if required to do so immediately. While 70 percent of companies have identified an emergency candidate to fill in as CEO on an interim basis, board members estimate that it would take 90 days, on average, to name a permanent successor. This may be due in part to the fact that boards do not spend extensive time discussing CEO succession. The same survey finds that boards dedicate only *2 hours per year* to the topic.[22] These are troubling statistics that suggest that some boards might not be fulfilling this specific duty to shareholders.

DEATH OF A CEO

Consider the following examples. When Jai Nagarkatti, CEO of Sigma-Aldrich, died of a heart attack in November 2010, his successor was announced the *next day*. Rakesh Sachdev, who previously had been chief financial officer of the company, became CEO and at the same time was elected to the board of directors. By contrast, when Wendy's International CEO Gordon Teter died of a heart attack in December 1999, the company did not immediately name a successor. Founder and director Dave Thomas was appointed to oversee a five-person management council that supervised the company's operations while the board searched for a permanent replacement. It was not until March 2000 — *three months* later — that John Schuessler, head of U.S. operations and 25-year veteran of the company, was promoted to CEO.

There is no greater test of the viability of a company's succession plan than the sudden death of its CEO. Approximately seven CEOs of publicly traded companies die each year. The most common causes of death are cancer, heart attack, and stroke. Less frequent, although still significant, are deaths due to airplane, automobile, and other accidents.

Cause of Death	Number of Deaths (1978-2000)
Heart attack or heart failure	39
Cancer or other tumor	30
Stroke or brain aneurysm	28
Following brief illness or pneumonia	16
Auto accident, airplane accident, drowning, lightning, or fire	14
Following other long illness	12
Following surgery for unreported illness	2
Unknown or undisclosed cause	20
Total	161

Source: Borokhovich, Brunarski, Donahue, and Harman, The Importance of Board Quality in the Event of a CEO Death, *The Financial Review*, 2006.

A company with a well-developed succession plan maintains a list of potential candidates that the board can turn to in case of an unexpected transition. Candidates are often internal executives who have been trained for higher levels of responsibility and whose skills, experiences, and leadership qualities match the strategic, operating, and cultural requirements of the company. In some cases, primary candidates are executives at other companies, whom the board has maintained contact with and is prepared to approach when a transition is required. If the circumstances are appropriate, a permanent successor is named without delay. In some cases (such as a company in turnaround or one that is in the process of building managerial talent), an emergency CEO is put in place until a permanent successor is identified.

A company without an operational succession plan does not have a set of viable candidates to turn to and often starts the evaluation process from scratch. In this case, the transition period can be lengthy, lasting several months or longer. Such delays can have a direct, negative impact on company performance. Behn, Dawley, Riley, and Yang (2006) demonstrate a negative relation between the length of the succession period and the future operating results of a company.[23] The longer it takes for a company to find a replacement CEO, the worse the company tends to perform going forward. For this reason, companies should treat succession planning as a risk management exercise as much as a leadership or talent development process.

A company might reduce uncertainty by increasing disclosure of its succession plan. However, there is little evidence that shareholders value this type of disclosure. According to Institutional Shareholder Services, shareholder-sponsored proposals that would require companies to develop and disclose succession plans received only 27 percent support in 2011.[24] This suggests that, while investors expect companies to develop succession plans, disclosure might not be informative of whether these plans are viable.

DEATH AND GOVERNANCE QUALITY

The sudden death of a CEO also provides an (unfortunate) opportunity for insight into the general quality of the firm's governance. When a CEO passes away, two distinct events occur. The first is the announcement of the death itself. The second is the announcement of the successor. The price of a company tends to go down following news of a CEO's death if the CEO is seen as a strong leader or vital to the company; and it tends to go up if the CEO is seen as entrenched, a poor leader, or inhibiting a sale of the company. In this way, a *positive* stock price reaction implies the presence of *poor* corporate governance, while a *negative* stock price reaction implies *good* governance. The case is reversed for the announcement of the successor. A positive stock price reaction suggests that shareholders believe the board of directors has made the right hiring decision for the company, while a negative reaction suggests that shareholders disapprove of the board's selection or that the hiring decision makes it less likely that the company will be sold. (In some cases, the two announcements are concurrent. When news of the death and news of the appointment occur on the same trading day, it is difficult to determine which news is more salient in driving the market's reaction.) Below is a table that illustrates the stock market reaction to various CEO deaths.

Company	Death	Successor
Micron Tech Steven Appleton, 51 12 Years as CEO	Feb. 3, 2012 Plane Crash Stock: -2.8%	2 Days Later Internal Stock: -2.8%*
Sigma-Aldrich Jai Nagarkati, 63 4 Years as CEO	Nov. 13, 2010 Heart Attack Stock: -1.0%	1 Day Later Internal Stock: -1.0%*
McDonald's Jim Cantalupo, 60 1 Year as CEO	Apr. 19, 2004 Heart Attack Stock: -2.6%	Same Day Internal Stock: -2.6%*
Dana Corp. Joseph Magliochetti 4 Years as CEO	Sep. 22, 2003 Pancreatitis Stock: 1.6%	135 Days Later External Stock: -0.2%
Triangle Pharmaceutical David Barry, 58 7 Years as CEO	Jan. 28, 2002 Heart Attack Stock: 1.0%	189 Days Later External Stock: 0.7%
Atlas Air Michael Chowdry, 45 9 Years as CEO	Jan. 24, 2001 Plane Crash Stock: -4.9%	1 Day Later Internal Stock: -4.9%*

Company	Death	Successor
Park Place Entertain. Arthur Goldberg, 58 10 Years as CEO	Oct. 19, 2000 Bone Marrow Stock: -6.4%	4 Days Later Internal Stock: 0.9%
Herbalife Mark Hughes, 44 20 Years as CEO	May 21, 2000 Overdose Stock: -12.0%	16 Days Later Internal Stock: -3.2%
Wendy's Gordon Teter, 58 5 Years as CEO	Dec. 18, 1999 Heart Attack Stock: 0.3%	89 Days Later Internal Stock: -7.8%
Cott Corp. Gerald Pencer, 52 9 Years as CEO	Feb. 3, 1998 Cancer Stock: 8.1%	129 Days Later External Stock: 6.5%
Texas Instruments Jerry Junkins, 58 11 Years as CEO	May. 29, 1996 Heart Attack Stock: -1.8%	26 Days Later Internal Stock: -0.2%
McCormick Bailey Thomas, 63 2 Years as CEO	Jul. 14, 1994 Heart Attack Stock: -3.7%	5 Days Later Internal Stock: 1.0%

Note: An asterisk (*) indicates that the announcement of the successor occurred on the first trading day following the death of the CEO. Here, the stock market change reflects the *combined* reaction to the announcements of the CEO's death and the announcement of the successor.

Source: Research by the authors.

For example, when Gerald Pencer, CEO of Cott Corporation, died of cancer in 1998, the stock price increased by 8.1 percent. Pencer and his family owned a 29 percent stake in Cott, and his death was seen as a catalyst that would accelerate change or possibly lead to a sale of the company. When former Campbell Soup executive Frank Weise was named CEO of Cott five months later, the stock rose 6.5 percent. The appointment of Weise, announced concurrently with a $110 million investment from private-equity firm Thomas H. Lee, was viewed as a commitment to boost growth, with the potential for a sale of the company down the road.

KEY LESSONS. KEY QUESTIONS.

1. It is very difficult for shareholders to gain detailed information about CEO succession planning among the companies they have invested in. Although CEO deaths are rare, the sudden death of a CEO can provide insight into the quality of succession planning and governance of a company. Whereas some companies are able to appoint a successor immediately, others take weeks or months to do so. Boards should do the "reality check" on whether they truly have an operational succession plan in place.

2. Most of the replacement CEOs in the table above are internal promotions. Does this mean that the best candidates were internal executives? Or does it mean that these companies could not find external CEOs in a timely manner? Notice that external searches take considerably longer (four to six months) than internal searches.

3. If a firm has a "good" CEO, we expect the stock price to go

down following his or her unexpected death. What should board members do if the stock price *rises* after their CEO dies? What does this say about shareholder perception of the firm?

4. Should the board revise its succession plan if its CEO engages in risky hobbies (e.g., flying airplanes or racing motorcycles) or risky habits (e.g., smoking and excessive drinking)? Should disclosure to shareholders be different in such situations?

8 HP: THE CEO MERRY-GO-ROUND

The previous chapter includes statistics and examples to suggest that many companies are not prepared to replace their CEO in an emergency. To shareholders (and the general public) this seems incomprehensible. How could a company not *always* have a plan in place to name a new CEO?

Companies are generally unable to name a replacement CEO for any of four reasons. First, the board views CEO succession as an exercise in talent selection rather than an exercise in *risk management*. The former means that the board will consider new candidates only after it knows a transition (retirement, dismissal, or acquisition) is going to occur. This is how many labor markets work—you only look for an engineer when you know you need one—and it is perhaps understandable that directors would view the CEO labor market the same way. When treated as an exercise in risk management, however, the board will consider the full spectrum of when a transition might occur and plan for multiple scenarios. This includes maintaining a list of viable internal and external candidates who would be ready at different points in time (e.g., tomorrow, one year, three years, etc.) and ranking them in order of preference.

Second, the board might be unable to name a replacement CEO because the company's internal talent development process is inadequate. This occurs either because the CEO has not shown an interest in mentoring and developing direct reports or because the board of directors has not emphasized the importance of doing so. Without a deep bench of talent and a rigorous grooming process in place, the board will not view internal executives as viable candidates and will be unprepared when a resignation occurs.

Third, the board might be overly deferential to the current CEO. It can be difficult for the board to discuss the possibility of replacing the CEO, particularly when the CEO is sitting in the room and not open to having such a discussion. Even in executive sessions of the board (in which only independent directors are present), the board will not have a meaningful conversation without the cooperation of the CEO. The CEO has day-to-day working knowledge of his or her direct reports and unless the CEO buys into the concept of open, honest, and continuous dialogue about succession, the board will not have access to the information it needs to properly evaluate internal talent.

Finally, the board might be unable to name a successor because its members have not reached consensus about the skills and experiences required to manage the company. This is the most troubling reason, and one that potentially signals deeper governance problems at the firm. For example, it might be that the board does not have a clear understanding of the company strategy or that its members disagree on the future direction of the company. Without consensus on these basic issues, all other governance processes — such as performance measurement, compensation design, risk management, etc. — break down. This can have a severely negative impact on long-term performance.

In this chapter, we will examine a company where multiple breakdowns in succession planning have occurred: Hewlett-Packard. Over the past decade, Hewlett-Packard has had to deal with not one but several CEO transitions, all of which were unpleasant and in the public eye. As we will see, while each event had its own unique set of circumstances, they shared many of the common attributes listed above. Over time, the situation cascaded to the point where the long-term health of the company was at risk.

CARLY FIORINA (1999-2005)

In 1999, the Hewlett-Packard Company hired Carly Fiorina to be its CEO. It was a striking move in many ways. Fiorina was the first female CEO in HP's history and the first without a background in engineering. She was also an outsider, having spent her entire career at AT&T and Lucent Technologies, the equipment manufacturing division which AT&T spun off as a separate company in 1995. This was unusual because, since its founding in the 1930s, HP had always been led by an engineer groomed from within. Furthermore, Fiorina wasn't actually the CEO of Lucent prior to joining HP. The highest level she had attained was group president, responsible for sales and marketing. Although group presidents have tremendous responsibility, there is a difference between being second-in-command and having senior-most responsibility for the entire organization. Typically, when a company searches outside for a CEO, it recruits a CEO from another company.

The decision to bring in an outsider was championed by none other than outgoing chairman and CEO Lewis Platt, a 32-year veteran of HP who himself had been promoted to the top job in 1992. Platt believed that the company had grown complacent in recent years and that an outsider with a fresh perspective was required to bring about needed change. The company's consensus-driven culture, long a source of pride for encouraging collaboration among workers, was now seen as an impediment to growth. Although HP's revenues were increasing at a double-digit rate, this was still below the hyperbolic growth rates of fellow Silicon Valley high-fliers Cisco, Oracle, and Sun Microsystems.

Fiorina quickly moved to reenergize the company. She reduced the number of reporting units from 83 to 12 and consolidated back-office functions. She replaced the company's profit sharing program with a performance-based compensation system to encourage individual productivity. She also revamped HP's sales and marketing functions.

In the process, she drew plenty of attention. *Fortune* magazine put her at the top of its list of the "50 Most Powerful Women in Business," a position she retained for five years. *The Wall Street Journal* described her as epitomizing "an alluring, controversial new breed of chief executive officers who combine grand visions with charismatic but self-centered and demanding styles."[25] Whereas Lewis Platt had always travelled by coach for business meetings, Fiorina asked HP to purchase a $30 million Gulfstream IV for her use.

To many inside the company, the changes in culture, style, and drive were extreme. One executive explained, "The feeling was, here was Carly, who wasn't a long time in the HP culture, who doesn't understand our business and the HP Way, and doesn't understand our strengths, particularly in businesses that were viewed as so successful for so long."[26] Another stated more simply, "The HP we know is gone."[27]

Fiorina also sought to revitalize the organization through acquisition. Previously, HP had grown organically, through the development of proprietary technology discovered in its own research labs. However, Fiorina believed that HP required both scale and breadth of service offerings to compete with its largest competitors and that this could best be achieved through a major acquisition. To this end, in 2000, she announced a bid to purchase the consulting arm of PricewaterhouseCoopers for $18 billion. The deal, however, unraveled one year later following a precipitous decline in HP stock. (IBM later acquired the consulting division of PwC for $3.5 billion.)

Undeterred, Fiorina announced a new acquisition, this time of Compaq Computer for $25 billion in stock. Compaq was the second-largest producer of personal computers, after Dell, and a major supplier of servers. A combination of the two companies would establish HP as a market leader in computer hardware, which Fiorina believed would give HP the leverage it needed to compete successfully with competitors such as IBM in the enterprise systems market.

The deal, however, was controversial in two regards. First, analysts were not convinced that it made strategic sense. HP was seen as doubling down on the commoditized business of hardware manufacturing at a time when many believed it should focus on higher-margin activities such as software, services, and printing. An analyst summarized this line of thinking: "Two losers don't make a winner."[28] Wall Street seemed to agree with this assessment. HP stock traded down 30 percent on the news. Second, the deal was controversial in that it drew public opposition from Walter Hewlett, son of company co-founder William Hewlett and a member of the company's board of directors. Although he had originally voted with other board members to approve the deal, he subsequently changed his mind. In a written statement, Hewlett said that, "Given the lack of stockholder benefits, I believe the extensive integration risks associated with this transaction are not worth taking."[29]

Shortly thereafter and in a sort of one-two punch, David Packard Jr., son of the other co-founder David Packard, also came out in opposition to the deal. Packard issued the statement that, "For some time I have been skeptical about management's confidence that it can aggressively reinvent HP culture overnight—a culture that developed over many years and was thoroughly tested under all kinds of business conditions. While change is necessary and inevitable, it does not follow that every innovation is an improvement."[30] In an escalation of the matter, Walter Hewlett announced a proxy fight, which David Packard supported, to terminate the deal.

Opposition by these two men was significant not only because they were sons of the founders but also because the foundations that they controlled—the William and Flora Hewlett Foundation and the David and Lucille Packard Foundation—together held 15 percent of HP's stock. If Fiorina was to overcome this obstacle and close the deal, she would have to convince a large majority of the remaining shareholders to vote against these two prominent men and side with her.

The controversy led to a rare, public squabble between the company and its major shareholders, with HP's directors joining the fray. Richard Hackborn, former executive vice president of HP and board member, defended the deal, stating,

"The board thoroughly analyzed this transaction and unanimously concluded this is the very best way to deliver the value our shareholders expect."[31] He admitted, however, to originally sharing Walter Hewlett's skepticism: "We all had reservations. None of us was convinced that Compaq was the exact right answer from the start." Philip Condit, another director, said the merger is "certainly not without risk, but I think the opportunity outweighs the risk." Director Robert Knowling said that at first he was "neutral" to the idea, but over time came to believe it was an important way to improve HP's competitive position. And board member George Keyworth said that, "Very good people have tried to transform this company through organic growth, targeted acquisitions and the old way. I believe, this board believes, we have to take a big step."[32]

In the end, following months of vigorous lobbying of institutional shareholders by Fiorina, the merger was approved by the razor-thin margin of 51.4 percent to 48.6 percent.

The Compaq acquisition, however, did not prove to be the transformative event that Fiorina and the majority of the board envisioned. Before the merger, HP had forecast that the PC division of the combined entities would generate an operating margin of 3.0 percent in 2003. The actual figure came in at 0.1 percent. In 2004, it was only 0.9 percent. It seemed the prediction that "two losers do not make a winner" was right. Following a string of disappointing earnings reports, the board asked Fiorina for her resignation. Robert Wayman, chief financial officer of HP, served as interim CEO while the board undertook a formal search for a successor. Fiorina made the statement, "While I regret the board and I have differences about how to execute HP's strategy, I respect their decision."[33] She left the company with a severance package valued at $21 million.

MARK HURD (2005-2010)

The search for Fiorina's successor was led by a three-person subcommittee of the board, which included nonexecutive chairman Patricia Dunn and directors George Keyworth and Thomas Perkins. At the outset of the process, Dunn declared that the board was committed to the business strategy that Fiorina had put in place but that "looking forward, we think the job is very reliant on hands-on execution, and we think that a new set of capabilities is called for." When asked whether the company would consider internal as well as external candidates, Dunn responded, "We are not ruling anything out, but we are committed to a very thorough search for the most qualified candidate. We anticipate that it is an external candidate, but we don't know for sure."[34]

Ultimately, the company named Mark Hurd, former CEO of NCR, as chief executive. While a relative unknown in Silicon Valley, Hurd had a reputation for strong operations management and strict cost controls. Although he had never managed a company of HP's size (NCR had $6 billion in revenue at the time, compared to HP's $80 billion), he had a long track record of success. He described his management style as follows: "I believe in very engaged management. I personally like to understand how the businesses work. You've heard the term 'management by walking around.' I like to move through multiple levels of the company and I like my management to do that. Great companies have boards, CEOs, and management that all have one script."[35] Separately, he said, "I live by a code that I got taught very early in my career, that it's the company first, the employees second, and you're last."[36] For his vastly different management style, the press labeled him "the un-Carly."

True to his word, Hurd made aggressive changes to company operations. He announced a broad restructuring, including the layoff of 14,500 employees. He reduced management layers and eliminated the corporate sales group, reassigning workers to divisional groups (PC, printing, and enterprise) so that they would have deeper knowledge of the products they sold. To improve accountability, he gave executives more control over their budgets, and held them strictly accountable for performance. The company used the cash flow generated by reduced operating costs to fund a series of acquisitions, primarily in the software and services spaces. These included Mercury Interactive, Peregrine Systems, Palm, and Electronic Data Systems. The approach appeared to pay off. Over the next five years, HP's operating margins increased from 4 percent to 9 percent.

Stability at the company, however, did not last. The company was rocked by controversy, first at the board-level and then, a few years later, at the CEO-level.

First, the board. In 2006, Patricia Dunn announced that she would resign as chairman, following a series of events which came to be known as the "pretexting scandal." HP had long had trouble containing the release of confidential information regarding boardroom discussions. The problem stemmed from the Fiorina era, when sensitive discussions regarding strategy, leadership, and corporate structure were anonymously leaked to the press. To identify the source of the leaks, Dunn hired a private investigative firm. This firm in turn hired a subcontractor, which used a controversial technique called "pretexting" (pretending to be someone else) to obtain the private phone records of both HP directors and reporters. Although Dunn knew that phone records were being reviewed in the process, she was unaware of the method by which they were obtained. Still, the violation of personal privacy and ethical standards was seen as so great that Dunn was forced to resign. George Keyworth—prominent physicist and board member since 1986—was identified as the source of the leaks and was not renominated to the board at the following annual meeting. Despite the moves, trust at the board level was never fully reestablished.

In 2010, the company faced another scandal, this time when Mark Hurd was accused by a company contractor of sexual harassment. Although the charges were determined to be unfounded, a board-level investigation revealed that Hurd had submitted inaccurate expense reports, purportedly in an attempt to conceal his relationship with the woman. The board asked for Hurd's resignation. Director Marc Andreessen called the move "a necessary decision."[37] His opinion, however, was by no means universal. Board members Joel Hyatt and John Joyce advocated that Hurd not be removed immediately but instead remain at the helm until an orderly transition could be arranged. They argued that an abrupt resignation was "a reckless way to make a change" that would cause damage to shareholders.[38] Others felt that Hurd had not been entirely forthcoming with the board and could not be trusted to continue. The board split six to four on the decision, and Hurd resigned. Although uninvolved, Larry Ellison, CEO of Oracle, expressed his own opinion: "The HP board just made the worst personnel decision since the idiots on the Apple board fired Steve Jobs many years ago…. In losing Mark Hurd, the HP board failed to act in the best interest of HP's employees, shareholders, customers, and partners."[39] It wasn't idle criticism. Less than one month later, Ellison put his money where his mouth was and hired Hurd to be president of Oracle's hardware division, where Hurd would compete head-to-head with his former employer. Hurd left HP with a severance package worth $35 million. CFO Cathie Lesjak was named CEO on an interim basis.

LÉO APOTHEKER (2010-2011)
The search committee for Hurd's successor included Marc Andreessen, Lawrence Babbio, John Hammergren, and Joel Hyatt. The process was plagued from the start. The dispute over Mark Hurd's resignation lingered to such a degree that it impeded the search committee's efforts. According to one director, "There were so many hard feelings. It became difficult to conduct business in a civil manner."[40] Board members were not in agreement about whether an internal or external candidate was preferable. Despite the prestige of the Hewlett-Packard name, several highly talented external candidates were not interested in the job. According to reports, the search committee approached executives at NCR, IBM, and Microsoft only to be rebuffed because they did not want to follow in

Hurd's footsteps.

When the company named Léo Apotheker as CEO in October 2010, the announcement was greeted with a lackluster response from shareholders. A native of Germany, Apotheker was the former CEO of SAP where he had overseen somewhat unremarkable results. "It's not something I would have expected," said one analyst.[41] An opinion piece in the *Wall Street Journal* highlighted "the unsettling reality that Mr. Apotheker has never truly run his own show, having been SAP's solo CEO for less than a year before his abrupt resignation."[42] More striking was the news (not made public for another year) that not all members of the board had interviewed, or even met, Apotheker before he was given the position. One director explained: "I admit it was highly unusual, but we were just too exhausted from all the infighting." According to another, "Among the finalists, he was the best of a very unattractive group."[43] Shortly after Apotheker's appointment, four members of the board resigned: Joel Hyatt, John Joyce, Robert Ryan, and Lucille Salhany. They were replaced by five new directors: Shumeet Banerji, Gary Reiner, Patricia Russo, Dominique Senequier, and Meg Whitman.

Apotheker's tenure at HP was brief and disappointing. At first, he committed to continuing the strategy that Hurd had put in place. Later, he reversed course and announced drastic changes: the company would terminate its recent foray into tablet computing, sell or spin off its PC division, and purchase business-analytics company Autonomy for $10.25 billion — a price that was ten times revenue. The news triggered a 20 percent decline in HP's stock. Recognizing the tremendous investor dissatisfaction, the board of directors terminated Apotheker's employment. He was given a severance package worth $9.6 million, after only 11 months.

MEG WHITMAN (2011-)

This time, the board of directors did not form a search committee or name an interim CEO. Immediately following Apotheker's resignation, the board named director Meg Whitman as CEO. Director Ray Lane became executive chairman. Whitman promised to continue the basic strategy of the company, although she would review (and later reverse) the decision to spin off the PC division.

Many in the investment community were puzzled by Whitman's appointment. Although Whitman was well known in Silicon Valley for her tenure at eBay and her unsuccessful run for the California governorship, she did not have the experience managing a company in the enterprise technology space, nor had she managed a company of HP's size and complexity. Ray Lane defended the decision: "If we thought there was a better choice outside, we would have conducted the search." When asked whether the board would make further changes to shore up investor dissatisfaction, Lane replied: "This is not the board that was around for pretexting. This is not the board that fired Mark Hurd. This not the board that did everything you want to write about…. It's just like open season to write about this board. It's not this board, okay?"[44]

HP: Stock Price History and Selected Events

Note: Adjusted for stock splits.

Source: Center for Research in Securities Prices at the University of Chicago.

KEY LESSONS. KEY QUESTIONS.

1. Hewlett Packard is a somewhat extreme example of a company whose board has repeatedly failed to develop and implement a workable CEO succession plan. Their problem appears to be two-fold. First, the board has not demonstrated clarity and agreement on the company's strategy, business model, and culture. Second, the board has not always had a clear understanding of the skills and experiences required for a CEO to manage the company. Had the board reached agreement on these issues, in all likelihood it would have made better decisions about the right person to run the

company.

2. The Hewlett Packard example also illustrates what it means for CEO succession planning to be an exercise in risk management. Succession planning is a process that, when done properly, reduces the chance of large errors that cause turmoil and impede performance. In the case of Hewlett Packard, this type of planning appears never to have occurred.

3. For decades, Hewlett Packard turned to insiders for its CEO. Beginning with Fiorina that strategy changed, and every CEO appointed since Fiorina has also come from the outside. In explaining the decision to appoint an external candidate, boards often claim that there are no insiders who are "ready now." However, every executive who becomes CEO at one point had to make the transition having never done the job before, and it is the responsibility of the board to mentor him or her through this process. Is it appropriate for a company to repeatedly view internal candidates as inferior to external candidates? At some point, shouldn't the board look at the "viability" of candidates rather than whether they are "ready now"? Would Hewlett Packard's history have been different if it had groomed internal talent rather than repeatedly gone outside for a CEO?

APPLE: IS CEO HEALTH PUBLIC OR PRIVATE?

The previous chapters suggest that companies should think of CEO succession planning as a risk management issue as much as a talent selection and recruitment issue. To this end, shareholder groups and regulators have pressured boards in recent years to increase disclosure about their CEO succession plans. The SEC encourages companies to disclose information that will allow shareholders to assess whether the company might be "adversely affected due to vacancy in leadership."[45] While many applaud this move, it broaches the secondary question of what information to include in this disclosure and how extensive it should be.

This is particularly true for companies whose CEOs are experiencing health issues. Shareholders might value detailed disclosure on the health of the CEO because it helps them to make a reasoned assessment of whether or when a transition might occur. This information is almost certainly relevant to the market price of a stock. At the same time, health information is a personal matter. The CEO might not wish to disclose his or her condition to the public. Where should companies draw the line between too much disclosure and not enough?

The sensitivity of this issue and the tradeoffs involved were exemplified at Apple, where former CEO Steve Jobs faced numerous questions regarding his health and the impact that his sudden departure would have on the company.

In October 2003, Steve Jobs was first diagnosed with pancreatic cancer. The board of directors was notified of his condition, but no public announcement was made. The specific form of cancer was rare but considered treatable, with the majority of patients undergoing surgery experiencing a survival rate of more than ten years. On July 31, 2004, Jobs entered Stanford Hospital for treatment.

The following day, Jobs sent an email to all Apple employees stating that, "This weekend I underwent a successful surgery to remove a cancerous tumor from my pancreas....I will be recuperating during the month of August, and expect to return to work in September. While I'm out, I've asked Tim Cook [executive vice president of sales and operations] to be responsible for Apple's day to day operations, so we shouldn't miss a beat."[46] A copy of the message was distributed to the Associated Press. It was the first public disclosure of his condition. Given Jobs' strategic and visionary role at the company, it is not surprising that Apple stock fell 2.4 percent when trading resumed the next day.

The issue of Jobs' health resurfaced in June 2008, when he appeared noticeably thin at a public appearance. A company spokeswoman responded to inquiries by stating that Jobs had "a common bug.... He's been on antibiotics and getting better day by day and didn't want to miss [the event]. That's all there is to it."[47] When analysts asked for more information during an earnings conference call, Apple CFO Peter Oppenheimer declined to elaborate: "Steve loves Apple. He serves as the CEO at the pleasure of Apple's board and has no plans to leave Apple. Steve's health is a private matter."[48]

In January 2009, Apple released another letter from Jobs in which he explained that his recent weight loss was due to a "hormone imbalance." According to the letter, "The remedy for this nutritional problem is relatively simple and straightforward, and I've already begun treatment.... I will continue as Apple's CEO during my recovery."[49] Concurrently, the board of directors issued a statement that, "[Jobs] deserves our complete and unwavering support during his recuperation. He most certainly has that from Apple and its Board."[50]

Ten days later, however, the company announced that Jobs would take another leave of absence. According to Jobs, "During the past week I have learned that my health-related issues are more complex than I originally thought. In order to take myself out of the limelight and focus on my health ... I have decided to take a medical leave of absence until the end of June."[51] No elaboration was offered. Tim Cook, chief operating officer at the time, resumed leadership of the company. In the two-week period surrounding these announcements, Apple stock fell 17 percent.

Jobs returned to work as scheduled six months later. Two weeks prior to his return, however, news leaked that Jobs had received a liver transplant at a Tennessee hospital during his leave of absence. A company spokeswoman declined to comment other than to say, "Steve continues to look forward to returning at the end of June, and there's nothing further to say."[52] Doctors unaffiliated with the case explained that tumors associated with the pancreatic cancer that Jobs was originally diagnosed with often metastasize in another organ, commonly the liver. The hospital where Jobs received the transplant stated that his prognosis was "excellent."[53]

In January 2011, Jobs took a third leave of absence. In an email to employees, he explained that he would "continue as CEO and be involved in major strategic decisions" but that Tim Cook would be responsible for "day to day operations." Jobs would be back with the company "as soon as I can. In the meantime, my family and I would deeply appreciate respect for our privacy."[54] When asked for additional comment, an Apple spokeswoman replied, "We've said all we're going to say."[55]

Although Jobs appeared at product launch events in the spring and summer, he never returned in full capacity to his position at Apple. After officially stepping down for the final time in August, he passed away in October 2011.

PUBLIC REACTION

Experts disagree over the appropriateness of Apple's disclosure of Steve Jobs' health during this period. Warren Buffett, CEO of Berkshire Hathaway who himself underwent colon surgery in 2000, has stated that Steve Jobs' health was a disclosable item: "If I have any serious illness, or something coming up of an important nature such as an operation or anything like that, I think the thing to do is just tell Berkshire shareholders about it. I work for them. Some people might think I'm important to the company. Certainly Steve Jobs is important to Apple. So it's a material fact.... Shareholders are going to find out about it anyway so I don't see a big privacy issue."[56]

Jerome York, former director of Apple, told the *Wall Street Journal* that the company's concealment of Jobs' health "disgusted" him and that he wished he had resigned over the matter.[57]

Charles Elson, director of the Center for Corporate Governance at the University of Delaware, believes that the company's use of public capital requires full disclosure: "The public should know basically what the board knows. Transparency in this situation is very important. When you go public and take public capital, one thing you agree to is you have less of an expectation of privacy than you would otherwise have."[58]

Others disagree. Robert Crandall, former CEO of American Airlines, believes that the company had no obligation to disclose more than it did: "I think the fact of the matter is that the precise nature of Steve Jobs' illness is a matter for Steve and his family."[59]

Arthur Levitt, former chairman of the SEC, thinks it would have been "insensitive" to seek additional information beyond what the company provided: "Jobs going on medical leave sends a message to the market. An intelligent investor should know the risks of Jobs having a relapse. For the board to opine on what the extent of the illness is right now I don't think is really necessary."[60]

The law was also on the side of the company. External counsel advised Apple's board that personal privacy trumped disclosure obligations so long as Jobs was able to continue to perform his duties. The SEC opened inquiries into the matter in 2006 and 2009, but in both cases closed the inquiry without taking further action.

KEY QUESTIONS. KEY LESSONS.

1. CEO succession is not only a strategic and operating decision for the board of directors but also a risk management consideration. Shareholders want to be assured that companies have a real succession plan in place that mitigates potential downside to the organization and that the board has a firm understanding of the quality of potential successor candidates as well as their relative strengths and weaknesses.

2. The issue of what information a company should disclose regarding the CEO's health continues to be a controversial subject. Companies handle this issue in different manners, based on the best judgment of the individuals involved. Still, there is no clear answer. How extensive should this disclosure be? How should the board of directors weigh its obligations to shareholders against the personal privacy rights of the CEO?

3. The nature of Steve Jobs' condition was extreme. Should the board disclose other, less sensitive information regarding CEO behavior that might be material to the stock price? For example, what if the CEO is involved in a contentious divorce that distracts from day-to-day management of the company? What if he or she exhibits unusually high stress levels that may precipitate an early resignation? What if the CEO engages in hobbies that carry above-average risk? Do shareholders have the right to know this information? Where should the board of directors draw the line?

PART IV: EXECUTIVE COMPENSATION

In this final section, we examine an important and controversial element of corporate governance: compensation programs. A compensation program is designed with three objectives in mind. First, it is expected to *attract* the right individuals — those with the skills, experiences, and behaviors necessary to succeed in the position. Second, it must *retain* those individuals, so they do not leave to work at another organization more willing to pay them appropriate compensation for their talents. Third, it must *motivate* them to achieve outcomes that are consistent with the objectives of the position and the firm.

CEO compensation is no different from compensation granted to any other job function. If well designed, it will attract, retain, and motivate highly qualified executives to deploy corporate assets in a way that maximizes shareholder value. If poorly designed, it will either attract the wrong talent or encourage behaviors that are not in shareholders' interests. For example, it might encourage "excessive" risk taking or an emphasis on short-term rather than long-term results.

The compensation committee of the board is responsible for designing a compensation package that meets these criteria. The committee typically works in conjunction with in-house staff (such as the human resources department) and/or a third-party consulting firm to design a compensation program that is market competitive. This exercise usually involves evaluating the external labor market, benchmarking compensation against a peer group of companies in the same or similar industries, and evaluating the company's strategy and risk tolerance. From this data, a recommended compensation package is proposed and then approved by a vote of the independent directors of the full board.

Historically, shareholders have had very little say in compensation matters. In the past, they were only required to approve equity-based pay (such as stock options and restricted shares) because these dilute their ownership interest. With the recent enactment of Dodd-Frank, shareholder rights are expanded. Companies are now required to allow shareholders an advisory (nonbinding) vote to approve executive compensation packages. This is popularly known as "say on pay." While a failed say-on-pay vote does not require the board to change its CEO compensation program, significant shareholder opposition creates an investor relations headache that most companies wish to avoid. To that end, the board must not only take into account the economic considerations of the compensation package but also the potential reaction of external stakeholders, such as shareholders, the media, and activists who pay careful attention to pay figures.

How exactly does the board of directors weigh these considerations? What specific factors do they take into account in designing pay? On average, are CEO pay packages "correct"? We will consider these questions in the following chapters.

WHAT IS CEO TALENT WORTH?

Executive compensation is a topic that elicits strong emotions from both corporate stakeholders and the public. On the one hand are those who believe—*strongly*—that CEOs in the United States are overpaid. They cite as evidence the growing disparity between the total pay granted to CEOs and the compensation of the average worker. (These figures tend to be very imprecise and depend on the sample and methodology, but one recent estimate pegs this ratio at 343:1.[61]) Their solution is to encourage shareholder activism (primarily through proxy measures) to communicate disapproval to companies and compel a reduction in compensation levels or stricter performance-based features that more closely align compensation to financial and operating results. Some critics go so far as to suggest that CEO compensation be regulated at a fixed multiple of the average worker's pay.

On the other side of the debate are those who believe that chief executives are paid the going fair-market rate. They argue that if compensation levels are high among the largest U.S. corporations, it is simply a reflection of the demands of a position that requires considerable time, skill, and attention. For the most part, they advocate a hands-off approach and continued disclosure on compensation size and structure so that market forces can correct the mispricing of talent when it arises.

Researchers have taken various approaches to evaluating whether CEO pay levels are appropriate. Gabaix and Landier (2008) measure the relation between CEO compensation and company size. They find that although CEO pay increased sixfold between 1980 and 2003, the market value of the companies these CEOs managed also increased sixfold during this period. They conclude that "the rise in CEO compensation is a simple mirror of the rise in the value of large U.S. companies since the 1980s."[62] Similarly, Kaplan and Rauh (2010) compare the growth rate of executive compensation to the growth rate of other highly paid professionals, such as hedge fund managers, private equity managers, venture capitalists, lawyers and professional athletes. They find that pay among these groups all grew by roughly the same order of magnitude during the period 1994 to 2005. They conclude that CEO compensation has increased due to market forces that contribute to general wage inflation among highly paid professionals, and that extreme compensation growth has not been limited to the business world.[63]

The following tables list the compensation paid to the highest-paid CEOs, actors, actresses, musicians, and athletes in 2010. Note that they are all roughly in the same ballpark.

Highest Paid CEOs

Name	Company	Reported Pay
Phillipe Dauman	Viacom	$84,469,515
Ray Irani	Occidental Petroleum	76,107,010
Lawrence Ellison	Oracle	70,143,075
Leslie Moonves	CBS	56,859,166
Richard Adkerson	Freeport McMoRan	35,294,023
Michael White	DirecTV	32,932,618
John Lundgren	Stanley Black & Decker	32,570,596
Robert Iger	Walt Disney	28,017,484
Brian Roberts	Comcast	28,155,865
Alan Mulally	Ford Motor	26,520,515

Highest Paid Actors

Name	Earnings
Leonardo DiCaprio	$77 million
Johnny Depp	50 million
Adam Sandler	40 million
Will Smith	36 million
Tom Hanks	35 million
Ben Stiller	34 million
Robert Downey Jr	31 million
Mark Wahlberg	28 million
Brad Pitt	20 million
Robert Pattinson	20 million

Highest Paid Actresses

Name	Earnings
Angelina Jolie	$30 million
Sarah Jessica Parker	30 million
Jennifer Aniston	28 million
Reese Witherspoon	28 million
Julia Roberts	20 million
Kristen Stewart	20 million
Katherine Heigl	19 million
Cameron Diaz	18 million
Sandra Bullock	15 million
Natalie Portman	8 million

Highest Paid Musicians

Name	Earnings
U2	$195 million
Bon Jovi	125 million
Elton John	100 million
Lady Gaga	90 million
Paul McCartney	67 million
Black Eyed Peas	61 million
Justin Bieber	53 million
Toby Keith	50 million
Usher	46 million
Taylor Swift	45 million

Highest Paid Athletes

Name	Earnings
Tiger Woods	$75 million
Kobe Bryant	53 million
LeBron James	48 million
Roger Federer	47 million
Phil Mickelson	47 million
David Beckham	40 million
Cristiano Ronaldo	38 million
Alex Rodriguez	35 million
Lionel Messi	32 million
Tom Brady	31 million

Source: Equilar, Securities and Exchange Commission, *Forbes*, 2010

However, it is important to remember that demonstrating a correlation between executive compensation and factors such as firm size or the compensation of non-business professionals does not mean that pay levels themselves are correct. It still might be the case that CEO pay *on average* is too high or too low.

MEASURING THE VALUE OF CEO TALENT

The table below provides summary compensation figures for the largest 4,300 publicly traded U.S. companies. It includes both the total annual compensation paid to the CEO and the market value of their companies, with the data bucketed by company size.

Company Size	Company Market Value (Median Average)	Total Annual CEO Compensation (Median Average)
Top 20%	$8,596,000,000	$7,707,000
Next Largest 20%	$1,588,000,000	$3,357,000
Middle 20%	$506,000,000	$1,666,000
Next Smallest 20%	$156,000,000	$865,000
Smallest 20%	$26,000,000	$393,000

Source: Equilar, 2012. Calculations by the authors.

Two things immediately jump out from these figures. First, there is a very large discrepancy between the compensation paid to the CEOs of the *largest* U.S. companies and the compensation paid to the CEO of an *average* U.S. company. Whereas the CEOs of the largest companies (top 20 percent) earn approximately $7.7 million per year, the average CEO earns only $1.7 million — almost five times less. CEOs of the smallest companies earn only $393,000. These figures are substantially lower than the figures widely reported in the press and are not particularly outlandish.

Second, while it is true that the CEOs of the largest companies earn considerable compensation, the size of their enterprises is also truly enormous. The largest U.S. corporations have a median market capitalization of $8.6 billion. Annual compensation of $7.7 million represents only 0.09 percent of this market value.

Still, these data do not demonstrate that CEOs are "worth" what they are paid. How would you make such a determination? One approach would be to measure 1) how much value creation at a large corporation is attributed to the efforts of a single executive and 2) how much of this value creation should be offered as compensation for these efforts. While this is simple in theory, it is exceptionally difficult in practice.

Two factors in particular make this calculation difficult. First, even though theorists and practitioners agree that CEOs play a critical role in affecting firm performance, researchers have not been able to quantify this impact. For example, Thomas (1988) finds that CEOs are responsible for only 3.9 percent of the variance in performance among companies, while Mackey (2005) finds that the impact is as high as 29.2 percent.[64] The view that the board has on this issue will have a substantial impact on what they are willing to offer as reasonable compensation.

Second, there are no agreed-upon standards that dictate the percentage of value creation that should be awarded in compensation. Compensation practices vary widely across professional fields. For example, executives that manage private-equity backed companies receive, on average, 5.4 percent of the equity upside they create (through stock and options). A-list actors in Hollywood receive $10 to $30 million per film, plus 10 to 20 percent of gross profits. Music artists receive 8 to 25 percent of the suggested retail price of an album, a $0.08 performance royalty when a song is played live or broadcast, plus a percentage of the gross profit generated on tour. Similarly, in setting compensation for CEO talent, the board should target a payout in relation to performance. In this regard, the *structure* of the compensation contract will be as important as its overall size.

Finally, as mentioned above, executive compensation packages will not correlate perfectly with company size. The ten most highly paid CEOs do not run the ten largest companies. Still, executive compensation should correlate with value creation, if not every year at least over time. Unfortunately, observation suggests that this is not always the case. We should therefore expect to observe highly paid CEOs who are not worth their compensation, and low paid CEOs who are worth substantially more. This tends to be what we find in real life.

KEY LESSONS. KEY QUESTIONS.

1. Executive compensation is a topic that is filled with much rhetoric ("nobody is worth $20 million per year") but somewhat less critical analysis ("maybe some CEOs are worth $20 million per year while others are not"). More of the discussion should be focused on the actual observable impact that a CEO has on value creation and the amount of compensation that is reasonable, given his or her performance. This approach will allow investors to better understand which CEOs are worth the compensation paid to them and which CEOs are not.

2. Companies produce very lengthy disclosure about executive compensation packages in the annual proxy. However, they rarely produce *explicit* calculations of the actual value created by the CEO. Why not? Without this calculation, how can shareholders be assured that boards are making rational decisions regarding pay?

11 WHAT DOES IT MEAN TO "MAKE" $1 MILLION?

In 2008, Vikram Pandit became the CEO of Citigroup. Pandit had joined the company six months prior as head of investment banking after Citigroup purchased the hedge fund he managed, Old Lane Partners, for $800 million. Between the $165.2 million in proceeds Pandit accrued in the sale and the $40 million compensation package he was offered when promoted to CEO, the *New York Times* dubbed him "Citigroup's quarter-billion dollar man."[65]

Despite the headlines, however, Pandit never actually received this amount of money. By the time Pandit's share of Old Lane Partners was liquidated in May 2008, it was worth a fraction of the original value, and the nearly $40 million in restricted shares and stock options awarded to him at promotion were worth only $4 million when they vested years later. Over the three-year period 2008 to 2010, Pandit realized only *$1.5 million* in cumulative take-home pay.

As this example suggests, executive compensation figures are not always what they seem. Executive pay packages contain a diverse mix of cash and non-cash incentives, payable in one or multiple years and subject to accruals, estimates, and restrictions that often render their ultimate value quite different from their expected value. The SEC standardizes the manner in which compensation is disclosed to investors in the annual proxy. However, even there, compensation figures comingle forward- and backward-looking amounts, as well as fixed and contingent payments, that make it difficult for investors to understand what compensation has been promised to executives and what they eventually earn.

In this chapter, we will put clarity around this issue. First, we explain the various methods that an investor can use to calculate executive compensation. Next, we explain why an investor might prefer one method over another, depending on the question he or she is trying to answer. Finally, we point out the errors that can occur when the wrong calculation is applied to the wrong circumstance.

MEASURING EXECUTIVE COMPENSATION

There are three basic ways to measure executive compensation:

- *Expected compensation* represents the expected value of compensation promised to an executive in a given year. This includes the sum value of the salary, annual bonus, long-term cash plan, stock option awards, and restricted stock awards in the year they are granted. Because some of these elements are contingent on future outcomes (such as operating performance or stock price), their expected value must be estimated. The precision of these estimates will vary depending on the type of compensation award that is offered. For example, the expected value of a salary is known with a high degree of certainty, because it is delivered on a pro rata basis throughout the year based on a promised and fixed amount. The expected value of a cash bonus is typically known with less, but still some, precision because it falls within a range (minimum, target, and maximum) that is bounded by the achievement of predetermined objectives. The value of long-term incentives such as restricted stock, stock options, and long-term cash plans is known with far less certainty because these elements are subject to multi-year operating, financial, and stock price results that are unknown in advance. They must be estimated using probability-based or market-based models. They also tend to be the largest elements of the executive compensation plan.

- *Earned compensation* represents the total value of compensation that an executive "earns the right to keep" as cash is delivered and vesting restrictions removed. Salary and annual bonuses are earned over one-year periods. Long-term cash awards are typically earned only at the end of multiple-year periods. Equity awards are earned as they vest and their value depends on the price of the stock *on the vesting date*. Note that if the stock price has appreciated or declined materially since the original grant date, the earned value will differ considerably from the original expected value. In most cases, the total compensation earned in a year includes some compensation elements that were awarded in the *current* year and other elements that were awarded in *previous* years. That is, some of the money that an executive earns today is money that was promised long ago.

- *Realized compensation* represents the total value of compensation that an executive takes home as *cash* in a given year. For cash awards (salary, bonus, and long-term cash plans), the earned value is the same as the realized value. For equity awards, the realized value is the amount of cash received when the executive ultimately sells shares or exercises and sells stock options. If the executive cashes out these pay elements on the vesting date, the realized amount will equal the earned amount. If the executive holds equity awards beyond the vesting date, the realized amount will be higher or lower than the earned amount, depending on whether the stock price subsequently increased or declined. Earned equity compensation that is retained after the vesting date, therefore, remains "at risk" until it has been sold. Like earned compensation, realized compensation often comprises pay elements awarded over multiple years and the realized amount is a function of firm performance over this period. The table below summarizes these differences:

Three Calculations of Executive Comp

Compensation Element	Expected	Earned	Realized
Salary	Target amount	Actual amount	
Cash Bonus	Target amount	Actual amount	
Restricted Stock	Value at grant	Value at vesting	Value at sale
Stock Options	Value at grant	Value at vesting	Value at sale
Long-Term Cash Plans	Target amount	Actual amount (lump sum)	
Pension	Actuarial amount		Actual amount
Other Benefits	Actual amount		

Source: The authors.

So which of these is the "right" measurement? The answer depends on what it is that you are trying to calculate. Expected compensation is a forward-looking view of the rewards available to an executive. It therefore provides insight into the *incentive* value of compensation. By contrast, earned and realized compensation are backward-looking views of the rewards that an executive actually received for his or her efforts, with earned compensation still somewhat "at risk" and realized compensation entirely "cashed out." These values can be compared to corporate performance during the measurement period to assess the relative *pay for performance* in the compensation plan. When compensation contracts consist heavily of equity-based awards and long-term cash plans, we tend to find that earned and realized compensation are highly correlated with performance. (They only pay out if performance exceeds company targets or the stock price goes up). When compensation contracts do not vary with accounting- and stock-based performance, the plan does not offer pay for performance.

Unfortunately, the information to assess the incentive value of compensation and pay for performance is not readily available to shareholders. This is because expected, earned, and realized compensation in a given year are rarely disclosed to the public. Although comprehensive information is mandated by the SEC and included in the annual proxy, it is not explicitly summarized along the dimensions discussed above. Instead, the annual proxy contains a Summary Compensation Table that commingles these figures. The investor must comb through the explanatory notes to calculate compensation according to the desired method.

SEC Guidelines for Reporting Comp

Compensation Element	Reported in the Annual Proxy
Salary	Earned, Realized
Cash Bonus	Earned, Realized
Restricted Stock	Expected
Stock Options	Expected
Non-Equity Plans	Earned, Realized
Pension	Expected, Earned
Other Benefits	Expected, Earned, Realized

The biggest mistake that an investor can make, therefore, in calculating executive compensation is to confuse expected, earned, and realized amounts. Investors should always keep in mind that the dollar amount promised might never be realized and that the dollars realized might be very different from what was originally promised. This is illustrated by the following example.

Harley Davidson, CEO Keith Wandell, 2010

	Expected	Earned
Salary	$ 975,000	$ 975,037
Bonus	0	0
Stock Awards	1,381,199	0
Option Awards	1,636,681	698,906
Non-Equity Plans	2,600,357	2,340,090
Pension	0	0
Other Benefits	83,490	83,490
Total	$ 6,676,727	$ 4,097,523
	Realized	**Annual Proxy**
Salary	$ 975,037	$ 975,037
Bonus	0	0
Stock Awards	0	1,381,199
Option Awards	0	1,636,681
Non-Equity Plans	2,340,090	2,340,090
Pension	0	0
Other Benefits	67,289	83,490
Total	$ 3,382,416	$ 6,416,498

Source: Securities and Exchange Commission. Calculations by the authors.

Proxy advisory firms, which advise institutional investors how to vote items on the annual proxy, do not clarify the matter. For example, in deciding whether to support a company's executive compensation plan, Institutional Shareholder Services (the largest proxy advisory firm) compares the year-over-year change in mostly *expected* compensation to *previous* one- and three-year total shareholder return. This approach is flawed because it takes a compensation figure that is predominantly forward-looking and compares it to backward-looking stock-price changes. A more reasonable approach would be to compare the change in *earned* compensation to the change in stock-price during the same measurement period.

Finally, journalists do not consistently distinguish between expected, earned, and realized compensation. For example, a recent article in the *New York Times* reported that Viacom CEO Philippe Dauman received total compensation of $84.5 million in 2010, more than twice the amount awarded the previous year. The article quoted a compensation consultant as stating, "This is spectacular money but where are the spectacular results?" Noting that the company's stock price had barely moved in three years, he asked: "Is that really worth this award?"[66] Had the article reported Dauman's compensation on an *earned*, rather than *expected*, basis the numbers would have looked quite different. Rather than report a 150 percent increase in compensation from $34 million to $84.5 million, the article would have shown a 26 percent increase from $17.2 million to $21.6 million. Furthermore, one-quarter of the nearly 500,000 options that Dauman had been awarded in previous years vested out-of-the-money in 2010, indicating that unless he subsequently increased the stock price he stood to earn no value from these awards, despite the fact that they were originally reported with an expected value of more than $7 million. Similarly, much of the $84.5 million in compensation granted to Dauman in 2010 was in the form of stock options and performance units, suggesting that their future value would depend heavily on his ability to increase shareholder value.

Viacom, CEO Philippe Dauman, 2009 and 2010

	2010 Reported	2010 Earned
Salary	$ 2,625,000	$ 2,625,000
Bonus	0	0
Stock Awards	41,833,309	5,919,015
Option Awards	28,620,000	1,599,827
Non-Equity Plans	11,250,000	11,250,000
Change in Pension	45,793	45,793
All Other	141,206	141,206
Total	$ 84,515,308	$ 21,580,841
	2009 Reported	**2009 Earned**
Salary	$ 2,500,000	$ 2,500,000
Bonus	0	0
Stock Awards	12,688,932	1,869,227
Option Awards	5,999,997	0
Non-Equity Plans	12,540,000	12,540,000
Change in Pension	37,911	37,911
All Other	243,150	243,150
Total	$ 34,009,990	$ 17,190,288

Source: Securities and Exchange Commission. Calculations by the authors.

This article is but one example of the confusion that is prevalent between the incentive that expected compensation provides for future performance and the rewards that earned compensation offers for previous results.

KEY LESSONS. KEY QUESTIONS.

1. Executive compensation figures are frequently cited by the press and others. However, these sources rarely distinguish between expected and earned compensation. It is important that shareholders understand the distinction between compensation that is offered and compensation that is ultimately received if they truly want to understand how much a CEO "made" in a given year.

2. In this chapter, we have shown examples of expected, earned, and realized pay for the same executive in a given year. In the case of Harley Davidson CEO Keith Wandell, these differed by almost 50 percent. In the case of Viacom CEO Philippe Dauman, they differed by almost 75 percent. Why don't companies voluntarily disclose all three of these figures so corporate stakeholders can more readily assess both the incentive value of compensation and pay for performance?

3. The previous chapter listed the compensation of the ten most highly paid CEOs in 2010. However, those figures were based on compensation amounts as reported in the annual proxy. It might very well turn out that these executives earn a lower amount when this compensation is realized in future years. If that is the case, it is likely that they were not actually the ten most highly paid CEOs of 2010. Only time will tell.

NETFLIX: EQUITY ON DEMAND

In the previous two chapters, we provided an overview of high-level issues relating to executive compensation. We emphasized that CEO pay levels should be considered in relation to the value that the CEO has created. We also outlined various methods of calculating executive compensation and showed that expected compensation can be used to evaluate the incentive value of pay, while earned or realized compensation can be used to evaluate the relation between pay and performance.

In this chapter, we broaden the discussion and consider how compensation plans fit into an organizational context. We examine how compensation plans can be used to support organizational goals by motivating employees to engage in behaviors that are consistent with the company's strategy, work processes, and culture. We will see that alignment between compensation and corporate objectives is critical to a well-functioning organization. To illustrate these points, we will use the example of Netflix.

CULTURE AND EMPLOYMENT PRACTICES

Netflix competes in the home entertainment industry, an industry characterized by continuous change and technological innovation with content providers, cable, satellite, internet, and technology companies all jockeying to develop new methods of service. To remain successful, Netflix relies on a dedicated workforce and high-performance culture to develop creative solutions and combat the "known obsolescence" inherent in its business.

CEO Reed Hastings describes that Netflix culture as encouraging "freedom and responsibility."[67] The company expects its employees to work hard, take ownership, show initiative, and act like owners by putting the company's interests first. In return, Netflix affords them considerable flexibility in how they perform their duties. The company minimizes the rules and bureaucracy that might inhibit their performance. A former marketing manager describes the company as having a "fully formed adult" culture.[68]

In hiring, the company targets high-performance employees who are capable of doing the work of two or three people. According to Hastings, "We endeavor to have only outstanding employees. One outstanding employee gets more done and costs less than two adequate employees." To attract these individuals, the company is willing to pay top-of-market wages. Netflix does not want a talented employee to leave the company to work elsewhere in a similar position for the same or higher wage. The company's philosophy is, "Pay them more than anyone else likely would. Pay them as much as a replacement would cost. Pay them as much as we would pay to keep them if they had a higher offer from elsewhere."[69]

In return, the company is demanding in its expectations for on-the-job performance. Only the highest-performing employees are retained. All others are let go so that their positions can be made available to more effective replacements. According to Hastings, "At most companies, average performers get an average raise. At Netflix, they get a generous severance package."[70] As a result, involuntary turnover at the company is very high — nearly *double* the industry average — while voluntary turnover is substantially lower. See the following table.

Turnover Statistics

	Silicon Valley Average	Netflix
Average annual total employee turnover	18 – 20 %	16 – 28 %
Average annual voluntary employee turnover	10 – 13 %	3 – 14 %
Average annual involuntary employee turnover	6 – 10 %	14 – 20 %

Sources: Netflix, 2007-2009; Compensia, 2008.

Netflix uses the review process to take a fresh look at an individual's performance and compensation each year. The company does not budget annual raise pools, in which employees receive a cost-of-living adjustment or merit-based increase. Instead, managers consider the most recent market data on compensation, and if necessary, the salary is adjusted to reflect current conditions — no matter the increase. Netflix applies the same methodology in the annual review as it does upon initial hire, with employee compensation set at the top-of-market rate. This practice reassures employees that they are *always* receiving a competitive wage. It also reinforces Netflix's willingness to fight to retain top performers.

The company's culture of "freedom and responsibility" is also emphasized through the company's vacation policy. The company does not track vacation time. Instead, employees are granted unlimited vacation during the year, with the expectation that they take only the time that they need. Patty McCord, chief talent officer at Netflix, explains: "When you have a workforce of fully formed professionals who have been working for much of their life, they understand the connection between the work they need to do and the time it takes to do it. You don't need to have a clock-in and clock-out mentality."[71]

Netflix also gives employees discretion to determine their own *mix* of compensation. While compensation is set at top-of-market rates, the percent of compensation that is awarded in cash versus stock options is largely at the discretion of the employee. If an employee is to receive total compensation of $100,000, he or she can request to receive the entire amount in cash, 50 percent cash and 50 percent stock options, or some other mix (up to a maximum 60 percent in stock options). While the company retains discretion to lower the requested stock compensation (and correspondingly increase the cash compensation) if necessary, such an override is rarely exercised.

This "cafeteria style" approach to compensation—giving employees a *choice* in how they want to be compensated—is highly unique. Hastings believes that the company's compensation practice is more economically efficient and provides better incentive value for performance. To understand why, we need to briefly explain how stock options work.

THE ECONOMICS OF STOCK OPTIONS

Employee stock options are contracts that give employees the right, but not the obligation, to purchase company stock at a predetermined price over the life of the contract. Most employee stock options carry a 10-year term and are granted with an exercise price equal to the price of the stock on the date of the grant (referred to as *at the money*). Typically, employee stock options carry restrictions that limit the ability of employees to exercise them immediately. For example, stock options usually vest in predetermined allotments (for example, 25 percent vesting every year for four years), and only once they have vested are employees free to exercise them. The board of directors determines the terms of the company's employee stock option program, and plans must be approved by shareholders.

An employee realizes value from a vested stock option by exercising it when the price of the stock is higher than the exercise price of the option. For example, if an option has an exercise price of $20 and the stock is trading at $25, the employee can realize a profit of $5 — the difference between the two, which is known as its *intrinsic value* — by exercising the option. The potential benefit that an employee realizes from a stock option award is a function of the firm's future stock price movement (the *time value*). If the employee believes that the stock price will go higher, he or she might wait to exercise the option at a later date. Otherwise, the employee might exercise the option early to lock in current profit.

In addition to a vesting requirement, employee stock options typically carry a termination restriction. Employees who voluntarily resign or are involuntarily terminated by the firm are typically given a 60-to-90-day window to exercise all vested, in-the-money options. Any options that are not exercised within this time frame are forfeited.

Because the value that the employee ultimately realizes from the option is unknown at the grant date, the company must estimate the cost of the option using an approved valuation method. This is the "expected value" that we discussed in the previous chapter. Many companies value options using the Black-Scholes pricing model, which relies on expectations about future stock price volatility, interest rates, dividends, and number of years until exercise to arrive at an estimated value. For example, in a normal market environment, a stock option for shares in a technology company that are currently trading near $20, with an exercise price of $20, might have a Black-Scholes valuation of $8.

Still, offering stock options as part of the compensation mix might be less economically efficient than offering the same amount in cash. This is because the perceived value of a stock option to an employee tends to be much lower than its mathematically calculated Black-Scholes value. Stock options are "at risk" compensation, their value is not guaranteed, and employees demand a premium when "at risk" compensation is substituted for guaranteed cash. Some studies suggest that the size of this premium is in the order of 100 percent (i.e., employees demand twice as much in stock option value to compensate for forfeited cash).[72]

Furthermore, other behavioral and economic factors reduce the value of stock options relative to their originally expected value. Employees who hold stock options tend to exercise them well before expiration. For example, employees holding 10-year options might exercise them after only five years, on average. When they do so, the employees forfeit the remaining time value of the options—even when value is significant. They do so either because they have anchored on a specific price at which to exercise their options (e.g., when the stock doubles), because they need the money to support their day-to-day living expenses, because they do not want to assume the risk that the stock will go down, or because they have underestimated the remaining time value of the option. Finally, the economic value of stock options decrease if the employee is forced to exercise them early or forfeit them following voluntary or involuntary termination from the firm. These factors are not easily accounted for in the "expected value" of an option, but they can significantly reduce its economic efficiency and incentive value.

So, why offer stock options at all? The incentives that stock options produce in terms of employee performance can be large. When offered appropriately, stock options produce economic returns for shareholders that more than compensate for the risk premium they require. Also, stock options encourage behavior—innovation, risk-taking, and alignment with company objectives—that might not be achievable through cash compensation alone.

COMPENSATION AT NETFLIX

Netflix has devised a unique approach to compensation that allows the company to benefit from the incentives that stock options can provide while not granting them to employees who do not properly value them. The key components of this system are as follows:

– *Compensation Mix*: At the end of each calendar year, exempt employees at Netflix are allowed to request *their own personal compensation mix* for the following year. Rather than have the company make this election for them, employees are given a total compensation amount and allowed to allocate it between base salary and options in the manner they feel is best for them (up to a maximum of 60 percent in options). At the end of the year, employees can change their allocation for the subsequent year; however, changes to the allocation during the course of the year are not allowed.

— *Pricing:* Option grants are made monthly, with one-twelfth of the annual allocation granted and priced on the first trading day of each month. The number of shares underlying each monthly allocation is calculated using the formula:

> Number of shares = monthly allocation ÷
> (stock price on grant date * 25 percent)

This formula is meant to provide a very generous valuation for the employee—a roughly 50 percent discount relative to the Black-Scholes calculation. (The company expenses the full value of the award on its income statement, as required by GAAP.) This means that an employee who gives up $1,000 per month in cash is granted options worth approximately $2,000 in expected value.

— *Vesting:* No vesting restrictions are attached to stock option awards. All stock options vest *immediately* and are exercisable as of the date of the grant. Management believes that vesting restrictions create a perverse incentive that encourages disengaged employees to remain at the company until their next tranche of options vests. According to one director, "If they're just there because they have a 'golden handcuff' for four or five years, that's not a productive employee. That's not an employee who's working for today. We don't incent people to hang on. We incent people to perform now."[73]

– *Termination*: The company does not require an employee to exercise vested options if the employee is terminated. Instead, former employees—both those who voluntarily resign and those who are fired—are allowed to hold unexercised options for the remainder of the entire 10-year term. The company believes that post-termination forfeiture is inappropriate, because employees have elected to give up salary that they had properly earned in exchange for options.

– *Cash Bonuses*: The company does not offer cash bonuses. Annual compensation is calculated to include the total value of salary and cash bonus that the employee would receive at a competitive firm. The company believes that a practice of no cash bonuses is consistent with its high-performance culture.

The Netflix approach to compensation is highly unique and intended to solve traditional problems relating to the economic efficiency and incentive value of compensation. At the same time, the program is designed to support the company's strategy, business model, and culture of "freedom and responsibility." Employees can choose the compensation mix that is right for them, they know that they will not forfeit option value if they resign or are terminated, and they recognize that they are always receiving compensation that is competitive with what they would receive at other firms.

KEY LESSONS. KEY QUESTIONS.

1. A well designed compensation program is intended to attract, retain, and motivate a specific profile of employ-

ee talent. To be successful, the company should design a compensation program that supports its strategy, business model, and culture. In this regard, both the size and mix of compensation are important. A compensation program that does not take these into account will not offer the right incentives to support the organization's goals.

2. Culture is an important factor in motivating employee behavior. The compensation program can play an important role in shaping culture by rewarding and reinforcing behaviors that are valued by the company and its shareholders. Risk tolerance, time horizon, effort, and ethical behavior are all influenced (positively or negatively) by compensation design.

3. The Netflix compensation plan is tailored to work in a fast-paced, highly dynamic industry that requires risk taking and employee dedication. To date, a plan with these features (cafeteria style approach to mix, immediate vesting, no forfeiture upon termination, etc.) has not been broadly adopted by other companies. Why not? Would it be effective in other settings?

CONCLUSION

Throughout this book we have attempted to provide a concise and accessible summary of corporate governance issues from a "real world" (rather than theoretical) perspective. We have explored issues relating to the board of directors, accounting and internal controls, CEO succession planning, and executive compensation, all from the perspective of understanding what does and does not work in organizational settings. Rather than prescribe "one-size-fits-all" solutions, we have tried to explain the trade-offs inherent in corporate decisions and isolate the key factors on which those decisions hinge. In doing so, we hope you have gained a better appreciation for the complex issues that directors, managers, shareholders, and regulators are faced with as they consider what corporate governance structures and standards to employ in their firms.

The key lessons of the book are summarized as follows:

First, the individuals elected to the board of directors must be qualified and engaged. Directors are elected to represent the interests of shareholders in overseeing and advising management. To be successful, they must have the requisite skills, knowledge, and professional background to help management and the board make correct decisions in the long-term interest of the company. As important as this is, it can be difficult for outside observers to assess the quality of a company's directors either individually or as a whole. Board quality cannot be captured through observable metrics, such as size, structure, or composition. Nor can it be captured through formal independence standards, which—though important—have not succeeded in delivering a litmus test that accurately weeds out directors who lack the objectivity necessary to represent shareholder interests. To evaluate board quality, a case-by-case analysis is required.

Second, the accuracy of financial statements relies on more than just the integrity of the accounting system. It relies on the integrity of the entire organizational system. The rules for describing corporate results are complex and their correct application requires the sound judgment of management. While internal controls are important to safeguarding these results from manipulation or fraud, these controls can only be so effective. If management or employees are intent on getting around them, they will. To prevent this, broad organizational factors—such as culture, leadership, "tone from the top," and a sense of ethical standards—must also come into play. Lord Oxburgh of Royal Dutch Shell was not correct when he said that the company's reserve problem lay in "human failings, not structural deficiencies." It lay in *both* human failings *and* structural deficiencies. The two cannot be separated.

Third, CEO succession planning is critical to the long-term success of any organization. To be effective, succession planning should be a continuous and ongoing activity within the firm. It is not a one-off decision that periodically arises whenever a CEO resigns, dies, or is fired. It is a continuous consideration as the board evaluates the skills and experiences required for the company to execute against its strategy now and in the future. An effective succession plan must be tied to the company's internal talent development program. It is the role of management to mentor and groom successors and the duty of the board to ensure that this happens. This is required of any responsible system that is expected to last beyond its current leadership. Only in extreme circumstances or if the company requires dramatic change should the board go outside for a successor. The frequency with which outside executives are chosen is testament to the fact that many boards likely fall short in this area.

Finally, compensation is a vitally important tool that corporate managers and directors use to motivate employees to perform. When designed correctly, compensation packages will attract, retain, and motivate employees to pursue activities that are aligned with the company's strategy and consistent with its tolerance for risk. This is true up and down the organizational chart, from hourly employees to the CEO. A compensation package—both its size and structure—should be considered in the context of the value it delivers. Prospectively, the expected value of compensation provides insights into the incentive that compensation offers. Retrospectively, earned and realized compensation offer insights into whether the plan offers "pay for performance." Compensation should also be evaluated in terms of its impact on risk taking and culture. Only when all of these factors are understood can we determine whether a pay package is "correct."

Given this, it is clear why "one-size-fits-all" governance solutions do not work. The honest evaluation of a corporate governance system requires an in-depth analysis of the company and its specific situation. This is true not only for the board of directors, but also for policies relating to internal controls, succession planning, and executive compensation. One-size-fits-all solutions do not work, because corporations are not monolithic entities. They must be fitted to their environment and the optimal adaptation will depend on local conditions. Governance "experts" who do not appreciate this clearly underestimate the complexity of the corporate world. The best solutions for governance problems can only come from well informed corporate stakeholders with a deep and honest understanding of its issues. For this reason, the best solutions require a real look at real world corporate governance.

ADDITIONAL MATERIALS

Additional resources and supporting material for this book are available at:
www.gsb.stanford.edu/cldr/

Sign up to receive free copies of the Closer Look Series:
Email: corpgovernance@gsb.stanford.edu
www.gsb.stanford.edu/cldr/research/closer_look.html

David F. Larcker is James Irvin Miller Professor of Accounting at the Graduate School of Business of Stanford University and professor at the Stanford Law School (courtesy). He was previously the Ernst & Young Professor of Accounting at the Wharton School of the University of Pennsylvania and Professor of accounting and information systems at the J. L. Kellogg Graduate School of Management at Northwestern University. He received bachelor's and master's degrees in engineering from the University of Missouri–Rolla and a doctorate in business from the University of Kansas.

David is senior faculty at the Stanford Rock Center for Corporate Governance and Morgan Stanley Director of the Center for Leadership Development and Research. He is also a trustee of the Wells Fargo Advantage Funds.

David has published many articles and book chapters on topics such as executive compensation, corporate governance, measurement of intangible assets, and strategic business models. He received the Notable Contribution to Management Accounting Literature Award in 2001. He is the coauthor of *Corporate Governance Matters: A Closer Look at Organizational Choices and Their Consequences*. In 2012, he was named to the NACD Directorship 100 as one of the most influential people in the boardroom and corporate governance community. He has served as a consultant to numerous organizations on corporate governance and design of executive compensation contracts.

Email: dlarcker@stanford.edu

Brian Tayan is a member of the Center for Leadership Development and Research at the Stanford Graduate School of Business. He has written broadly on the subject of corporate governance, including studies and other materials on boards of directors, succession planning, executive compensation, financial accounting, and shareholder relations. He is the coauthor of *Corporate Governance Matters: A Closer Look at Organizational Choices and Their Consequences.*

Previously, Brian worked as a financial analyst at Stanford University's Office of the CFO and as an investment associate at UBS Private Wealth Management. He received his MBA from the Stanford Graduate School of Business and his BA from Princeton University.

Email: btayan@stanford.edu

ABOUT THE CENTER FOR LEADERSHIP DEVELOPMENT AND RESEARCH AT THE STANFORD GRADUATE SCHOOL OF BUSINESS

The Center for Leadership Development and Research mission is to advance the intellectual understanding of corporate governance and executive leadership by engaging academics, regulators, practitioners and professionals, bridging the gap between theory and practice. We aim to strengthen governance and leadership as independent areas of teaching and scholarship in business schools worldwide and to generate new insights into fundamental "big issues."

ENDNOTES

1   Carl C. Icahn, "The Economy Corporate Governance Reform," *The Wall Street Journal*, Jan. 23, 2009.

2   Steven M. Davidoff, "Corporate Governance Issues Grow More Complex," *The New York Times*, Oct. 21, 2011.

3   Sample includes 500 respondents including fund managers, bankers, analysts, and asset managers. Labaton Sucharow, "US & UK Financial Services Industry Survey," Jul. 2012.

4   Andy Serwer and Corey Hajim, "The Improbable Power Broker," *Fortune*, Apr. 17, 2006.

5   National Association of Corporate Directors (NACD) and The Center for Board Leadership, "2009 NACD Public Company Governance Survey" (2009).

6   Rüdiger Fahlenbrach, Angie Low, and René M. Stulz, "Why Do Firms Appoint CEOs as Outside Directors?" *Journal of Financial Economics* (2010).

7   Michael Santoli, "Totally in Control," *Barron's*, Aug. 16, 2010; and "Q3 2010 Johnson Controls Earnings Conference Call," CQ FD Disclosure, Jul. 23, 2010 (edited lightly for clarity).

8   M.T. Bradshaw, "Discussion of 'Assessing the Relative Informativeness and Persistence of Pro Forma Earnings and GAAP Operating Earnings", *Journal of Accounting and Economics* (2003).

9   Berkshire Hathaway, 2009 Annual Report. Available at: http://www.berkshirehathaway.com/reports.html.

10 Christopher Knowlton, "Shell Gets Rich by Beating Risk," *Fortune*, Aug. 26, 1991.

11 *Ibid.*, loc. cit.

12 Robert Corzine, "Man Bent on Effecting a Sea Change at Shell," *The Financial Times*, Aug. 8, 1998.

13 Michael Harrison, "Shell Profits Plunge in Worst Results on Record," *The Independent*. Feb. 12, 1999.

14 "Shell Cuts Reserve Estimate 20 percent as SEC Scrutinizes Oil Industry," *The Wall Street Journal*, loc. cit.

15 Quotations and timeline from: "Report of Davis Polk & Wardwell to the Shell Group Audit Committee, Executive Summary," Mar. 31, 2004.

16 Norma Cohen and Clay Harris, "Human Failings and Hyperbolic E-mails," *The Financial Times*, Apr. 20, 2004.

17 Martin Dickson, "Shell Shocked and Still Very Badly in Denial," *The Financial Times*, Apr. 20, 2004.

18 Transparency International, "Bribe Payers Index 2008." Available at: http://www.

transparency.org/news_room/in_focus/2008/bpi_2008.

19 The details in this section derived from: Securities and Exchange Commission, Accounting and Auditing Enforcement Release No. 1444, in the Matter of Baker Hughes Incorporated, Sep. 12, 2001. Available at: http://www.sec.gov/litigation/admin/34-44784.htm.

20 The details in this section derived from: Securities and Exchange Commission, Accounting and Auditing Enforcement Release No. 2602, "SEC Charges Baker Hughes with Foreign Bribery and with Violating 2001 Commission Cease-and-Desist Order," Apr. 26, 2007. Available at: http://www.sec.gov/litigation/litreleases/2007/ lr20094.htm.

21 The full case and settlement terms with the Department of Justice are reproduced in: Baker Hughes, form 10-Q for the quarter ending Mar. 31, 2007, Exhibit 99.3, Sentencing Memorandum and Motion for Waiver, filed with the Securities and Exchange Commission, Apr. 30, 2007.

22 Heidrick & Struggles and the Rock Center for Corporate Governance at Stanford University, "2010 Survey on CEO Succession Planning, Jun. 2010. Available at: http://www.gsb.stanford.edu/cldr.

23 Bruce K. Behn, David D. Dawley, Richard Riley, and Ya-wen Yang, "Deaths of CEOs: Are Delays in Naming Successors and Insider/Outsider Succession Associated with Subsequent Firm Performance?" *Journal of Managerial Issues* (Spring 2006).

24 Institutional Shareholder Services, "2011 U.S. Proxy Season Scorecard."

25 George Anders, "H-P Board Ousts Fiorina as CEO," *The Wall Street Journal*, Feb. 10, 2005.

26 David P. Hamilton, "Soul Saver: Inside Hewlett-Packard, Carly Fiorina Combines Discipline, New-Age Talk," *The Wall Street Journal*, Aug. 22, 2000.

27 Quentin Hardy, "The Cult of Carly," *Forbes*, Dec. 13, 1999.

28 Molly Williams, "H-P's Deal for Compaq Has Doubters As Value of Plan Falls to $20.52 Billion," *The Wall Street Journal*, Sep. 5, 2001.

29 Brian Bergstein, "Family, Foundation of HP Co-Founder Oppose Compaq Deal," Associated Press, Nov. 6, 2001.

30 Brian Bergstein, "Rebukes from Hewlett-Packard Sons Make Fiorina's Life Hard," Associated Press, Nov. 7, 2001.

31 Ibid.

32 Steve Lohr, "It's the Scion vs. the Board in Merger Fight," *The New York Times*, Feb. 4, 2002.

33 Pui-Wing Tam, "Fallen Star: HP's Board Ousts Fiorina as CEO," *The Wall Street Journal*, Feb. 10, 2005.

34 Edited lightly for clarity. "Hewlett-Packard Conference Call-Financial Analysts," FD (Fair Disclosure) *Wire*, Feb. 9, 2005.

35 Pui Wing Tam, "Boss Talk: Hitting the Ground Running—New CEO of H-P

Immerses himself in Studying Company," *The Wall Street Journal*, Apr. 5, 2005.

36 Adam Lashinsky and Doris Burke, "Mark Hurd's Moment," *Fortune*, Mar. 16, 2009.

37 Ashlee Vance, "Hewlett-Packard Ousts Chief for Hiding Payments to Friend," *The New York Times*, Aug. 7, 2010.

38 Ben Worthen, Justin Scheck and Joann Lublin, "H-P Defends Hasty Whitman Hire," *The Wall Street Journal*, Sep. 23, 2011.

39 Ashlee Vance, "Oracle Chief Faults HP Board for Forcing Hurd Out," *The New York Times*, Aug. 10, 2010.

40 James B. Stewart, "Ouster of Hewlett-Packard CEO is Expected: Most Voted to Hire Apotheker without Meeting Him," *The New York Times*, Sep. 22, 2011.

41 Ashlee Vance, "Ex-Chief of SAP is Named to Lead H-P," *The New York Times*, Oct. 1, 2010.

42 Rolfe Winkler, "Is Apotheker Right Potion for H-P?" *The Wall Street Journal*, Oct. 2, 2010.

43 James B. Stewart, loc. cit.

44 "Hewlett-Packard Names Meg Whitman President and Chief Executive Officer Conference Call," Sep. 22, 2011. Available at: http://h30261.www3.hp.com/phoenix.zhtml?c=71087&p=irol-irhome.

45 SEC Staff Legal Bulletin 14E (CF), "Shareholder Proposals." Oct. 27, 2009. Available at: http://www.sec.gov/interps/legal/cfslb14e.htm.

46 "Text of Message from Steve Jobs," Associated Press, Aug. 2, 2004.

47 Steven Russolillo, "Apple Says Bug Caused CEO's Frail Appearance; Concerns Remain," *Dow Jones Newswire*, Jun. 10, 2008.

48 Apple Inc., "Q3 2008 Apple Inc. Earnings Conference Call," *Voxant FD Wire*, Jul. 21, 2008.

49 Apple, Press Release, "Letter from Apple CEO Steve Jobs," Jan. 5, 2009, Available at: http://www.apple.com/pr/library/2009/01/05sjletter.html.

50 Apple, Press Release, "Statement by Apple's Board of Directors," Jan. 5, 2009. Available at: http://www.apple.com/pr/library/2009/01/05bod.html.

51 Apple, Press Release, "Apple Media Advisory," Jan. 14, 2009. Available at: http://www.apple.com/pr/library/2009/01/14advisory.html.

52 Yukari Iwatani Kane and Joann S. Lublin, "Jobs Had Liver Transplant," *The Wall Street Journal*, Jun. 20, 2009.

53 Yukari Iwatani Kane, "Memphis Site of Transplant for Jobs Liver," *The Wall Street Journal*, Jun. 24, 2009.

54 Apple, Press Release, "Apple Media Advisory," Jan. 17, 2011. Available at: http://www.apple.com/pr/library/2011/01/17advisory.html.

55 Yukari Iwatani Kane and Joann S. Lublin, "Apple Chief to Take Leave," *The Wall Street Journal*, Jan. 18, 2011.

56 Alex Crippen, "Warren Buffett: Apple Withheld 'Material Fact' on Steve Jobs

Health," *CNBC*, Jun. 24, 2009. Edited slightly for clarity.

57 Yukari Iwatani Kane and Joann S. Lublin, "On Apple's Board, Fewer Independent Voices," *The Wall Street Journal*, March 25, 2010.

58 Interview with Charles Elson, "Cavuto," *Fox News*, Jan. 17, 2011. Edited slightly for clarity.

59 Interview with Robert Crandall, "Cavuto," *Fox News*, Jan. 17, 2011.

60 Adam Satariano, "Apple Is Right on Jobs Disclosure, Former SEC Chair Levitt Says," *Bloomberg*, Jan. 20, 2011.

61 See AFL-CIO Executive Paywatch, available at: http://www.aflcio.org/corporate-watch/paywatch/.

62 Xavier Gabaix and Augustin Landier, "Why Has CEO Pay Increased So Much?" *Quarterly Journal of Economics* (2008).

63 Steven N. Kaplan and Joshua Rauh, "Wall Street and Main Street: What Contributes to the Rise in the Highest Incomes?" *Review of Financial Studies* (2010).

64 Alan Berkeley Thomas, "Does Leadership Make a Difference in Organizational Performance?" *Administrative Science Quarterly* (1988). Alison Mackey, "How Much Do CEOs Influence Firm Performance — Really?" (2005), available at SSRN: http://ssrn.com/abstract=816065.

65 As part of his employment agreement, Pandit promised to retain the after-tax proceeds of the sale as an investment interest in Old Lane. Source: Eric Dash, "All Told, the Price Tag for Citigroup's New Chief is \$216 Million," *The New York Times*, Mar. 14, 2008.

66 Graham Bowley, "Pay Doubles for Leaders at Viacom," *The New York Times*, Jan. 22, 2011.

67 Netflix, "Reference Guide on Our Freedom and Responsibility Culture," http://www.slideshare.net/reed2001/culture-1798664.

68 Michelle Conlin, "Rewards Netflix: Flex to the Max," *BusinessWeek*, Sep. 24, 2007.

69 Netflix, "Reference Guide on Our Freedom and Responsibility Culture," loc. cit.

70 Michelle Conlin, op. cit.

71 Ken Belson, "When Flexi Is Sexy," *Today*, Sep. 1, 2007. Edited for clarity.

72 See: Richard A. Lambert et al., "Portfolio Considerations in Valuing Executive Compensation," *Journal of Accounting Research* (1991).

73 Christina Fuoco-Karasinski, "Netflix Bucks Traditional Total Rewards," *Workspan*, Aug. 2007.

Made in United States
North Haven, CT
30 September 2022

24725741R00088